Character
Builders

Loveland, Colorado

Character Builders

Copyright © 1998 Group Publishing, Inc.

Credits
Contributing Authors: Katrina Arbuckle, Ivy Beckwith, Jody Brolsma, Robin Christy, Nancy Wendland Feehrer, Debbie Gowensmith, Mikal Keefer, Gina Leuthauser, Karl Leuthauser, Amy Simpson, Trevor Simpson, Helen Turnbull, and Paul Woods
Book Acquisitions Editor: Jan Kershner
Editor: Lori Haynes Niles
Creative Development Editor: Dave Thornton
Chief Creative Officer: Joani Schultz
Copy Editor: Julie Meiklejohn
Art Director: Kari K. Monson
Cover Art Director: Jeff A. Storm
Computer Graphic Artist: Eris Klein
Cover Photographer: FPG International
Cover Designer: Diana Walters
Illustrator: Christine Nuanez-Voegtle
Production Manager: Peggy Naylor

Library of Congress Cataloging-in-Publication Data
Character builders.
     p.   cm.
   Includes index.
   ISBN 0-7644-2061-5
   1. Christian education of children. 2. Christian ethics--Study and teaching.   I. Group Publishing.
BV 1457.2.G74 1998
268'.432--dc21
                                               98-12122
                                               CIP

10 9 8 7 6 5 4 3 2   07 06 05 04 03 02 01 00 99
Printed in the United States of America.
Visit our Web site: www.grouppublishing.com

Contents

Foreword

Developing conscience and character in a child is an ongoing task for each significant adult in the life of a child. In the past, character development was an intrinsic part of our culture. Parents were part of a bigger team. Home, church or synagogue, school, and clubs taught the same basic character traits and worked together to help children choose right instead of wrong.

Traditionally, we thought of developing character traits as instilling positive, constructive ideas and applications. We told Bible stories of heroes and heroines who modeled godly character traits we hoped our learners would choose. However, there has been a jolting shift in our culture in the past thirty years. Many of our modern-day heroes and heroines model violence and revenge as a way of life. Early childhood experiences are filled with media demonstrations of anger, revenge, and violence as the preferred ways to resolve conflict. Choosing destructive, negative character traits and value systems has become the way to peer acceptance and even gang membership.

As Christian educators and parents, we are obligated to rethink and clarify our ideas and definitions of character development. How can we combat negative influence on the conscience and character of our children? How can we be intentional about helping the children of America identify, clarify, and develop personal conscience and positive character?

We begin by identifying a common set of constructive foundation traits. Eight foundation traits which are based on God's character are:

- **compassion,**
- **forgiveness,**
- **integrity,**
- **respect,**
- **responsibility,**
- **initiative,**
- **cooperation,** and
- **perseverance.**

The next step is to clarify the definition of each of the traits and identify its opposite destructive trait. By contrasting the constructive and destructive aspects of each character trait, we gain a clearer perception of the specific nature of each trait. For example, the constructive trait **compassion** can be defined as "sympathy for someone else's suffering or misfortune, together with the desire to help."[1] When people build relationships on compassion, they are able to give each other the best they have. The opposite destructive trait is **indifference**: "a lack of interest, concern, or care; a lack of sensitivity or regard for others' needs or troubles."[2]

From these identified foundation traits based on the nature of God, other positive "outgrowth" traits develop. For example, the outgrowth trait **kindness** comes from becoming a person of **compassion**. **Obedience** has its roots in the foundation traits of **compassion**, **respect**, and **responsibility**. **Honesty** grows from **integrity**, but is also impacted by **compassion** and **initiative**. The values that develop as a result of these character traits become very personal and impact the way each individual uniquely relates to others and to society. (See "Progression From Traits to Values" below.)

PROGRESSION FROM TRAITS TO VALUES

Foundation Traits	Outgrowth Traits	Values
FORGIVENESS ➡	Humility Gratitude Joy Peace ➡	Serving Others Reconciliation Restoration Mercy
Compassion		
Integrity		
Respect		
Responsibility		
Initiative		
Cooperation		
Perseverance		

At this point in the process, parents, teachers, grandparents and significant adults need to learn to take these abstract concepts of character and recast them into concrete experiences by providing opportunities for children to actively participate in making choices and decisions and to experience the resulting consequences.* These experiences enable a child to understand the security, belonging, and worth that come from living out a life that is driven by positive character. In this context, children learn to discern right from wrong and then make right choices, even when no one is looking.

To facilitate concrete experiences, consider the following methods:

Readiness Activities help the learner get ready to think and learn about a specific topic. When working with the character trait **integrity**, for example, and more specifically the outgrowth trait of **promise keeping**, ask each child to draw a picture or write about a time when someone kept or broke a promise to him or her. Follow up with a discussion about promises and the choices a person of integrity makes when he or she keeps a promise.

Storytelling is a time-honored, favorite way to develop character. Stories teach by attraction rather than by compulsion. They invite rather than impose. Stories capture the imagination and stir strong feelings. Stories give hope and encouragement. They stir minds to think about other ideas and choices that are possible.

Tell the Bible stories associated with the activities presented in this book with enthusiasm! They are a gift from God and are useful for "training in righteousness" (2 Timothy 3:16).

Questions before and after stories allow children to begin to think and discuss the character traits and actions of the people in the story. Questions need to be brief, clear, and limited to one concept at a time. Make sure your questions are ones that are open-ended and cannot be answered with a single word (like "yes" or "no"!).

The structure of the questions presented in each activity in this book provides an example of the kind of additional questions you can ask to expand your learners' understanding.

Learning Activities are an effective method to develop and practice a character trait in the classroom. Children gain firsthand experiences that can be applied to their real-life challenges. Make sure to consider both the general age-characteristics and individual differences of your particular learners when you select an activity. Take into account the various interests, abilities and learning styles represented. Provide choices for expression whenever possible, allowing children to decide whether to write or draw, to speak or act out. Always help children apply a biblical truth or character trait to their own unique life experiences. Changed lives happen when learners apply the Bible truth and character trait to their daily lives.

As you prepare to teach, keep in mind these **Ten Big Ideas on Developing Character**:
- **Remember that children develop character slowly and in stages;**
- **Respect children, and require respect in return;**
- **Teach and develop character by example;**
- **Help children learn to think honestly;**
- **Help children assume real responsibilities;**
- **Balance high support and high control;**
- **Initiate and demonstrate forgiveness, regardless of blame;**
- **Love children! Love is vital for character development;**

- **Provide ways for children to make choices**; and
- **Ask questions instead of giving answers.**

Developing character is more than learning and changing behavior—it is changing of the mind, the spirit, and the will. My prayer is that you may *enjoy* being part of the development of character in the lives of the children you influence and surrender to God's development of **your** character as a part of the process.

Vernie Schorr
Children of the World
San Clemente, California

Character-education conferences and seminars are available to help adults learn how to help children think, ask questions, and discuss issues of choice and conflict. For more information, write Character Development Project, 501 N. El Camino Real, Ste. 218, San Clemente, CA 92672 or phone (714) 366-4134.

---

[1] Building Character, Children of the World, Unit Two, Compassion.

[2] Vernie Schorr, "Changing Perceptions of Character Education," News That Makes a Difference (October 1997).

Chapter One

Courage

The Cowardly Lion longed for it, Stephen Crane novelized it, John F. Kennedy profiled it, but children are faced with choices that require it every day. Courage is that essential character trait that allows an individual to press on rather than withdraw, to take a stand rather than give in, and to grow rather than wither. People who have courage can decide on a course of action and do what they know is best, even if it means acting alone.

Developing courage will enable kids to withstand peer pressure, apply their faith, and confront new challenges. But courage isn't some natural personality trait to be summoned when we need it. Courage is rooted in the unshakable belief that the same God who delivered Daniel and David from hungry lions is alive and present with us today. His power supercharges our effort and will help kids overcome any obstacle they'll meet.

● ● ●

Courage That Counts

Place a wastebasket at one side of the room, and have kids line up about fifteen feet away. Hold up a small, lightweight ball, such as a table tennis ball. Ask:

● **Do you think you can get the ball into the wastebasket from where you are standing?**

Give kids each two or three tries.

Say: **Remember whether you got the ball in every time, because now we're going to change the game a bit. The object is still to get the ball into the wastebasket, but I'm going to stand here next to it. You'll throw the ball to me, and I'll drop the ball in.** Have kids take turns tossing the ball to you. Drop the ball into the basket each time, even if you have to chase the ball down. Then ask:

● **Why did we do so much better getting the ball into the basket this time?**

Read aloud the story of David and Goliath from 1 Samuel 17:1-50, or have the kids summarize it. Specifically read verse 37. Then ask:

● **How is what happened in this story similar to what we did with the ball?**

● **What does David's story show us about how we can have courage?**

A Whole Lot of Shakin' Goin' On

Tie an eight-foot piece of rope to join the legs of two chairs.

Say: **In New York City, the World Trade Center is made up of two towers. Each tower is 110 stories tall. That's 1,350 feet from the street to the top of the towers. Let's pretend this rope is tied between the tops of the two towers.**

You've been asked to walk across this rope between the two buildings to prove your courage. Gusts of wind may shake the rope. You may lose your balance and fall to your death. A crowd has gathered to see what you will do. Ask:

● **What will you do? Why?**

Hold an imaginary microphone to the mouth of each child as he or she answers.

Say: **Now suppose you look across at the other tower. Standing on it are all the people you love—your family and your friends. The towers are beginning to crumble. Your family and friends are begging you to cross the rope to help them get down safely and save their lives.** Ask:

● **Now what will you do? Why? If you changed your mind, what influenced you to make that decision?**

Say: **Doing something dangerous doesn't mean you're brave. It may mean you're foolish! But doing something dangerous *for the right reason* takes courage. It takes courage to act to save lives, to share the gospel when others don't applaud, to stay honest when everyone else is cheating, or to tell the truth when others lie.**

Ask a student to read aloud 1 Corinthians 16:13-14. Ask:

● **Why does standing firm in the faith take courage?**

● **What's one way you can be courageous and stand firm in your faith this week?**

For a follow-up game, place the rope on the floor and ask children to attempt to walk the length of the rope, heel to toe. Then ask for volunteers to walk the rope again with their eyes closed. Provide a "spotter" during this second walk.

I Ain't Scared!

Have the children be seated in a circle. Starting with the child wearing the most yellow, ask children to make the scariest faces they can, one at a time. Go around the circle to the left.

After each child makes a scary face, lead the rest of the children in shouting, "I ain't scared!"

After children have each had a turn, ask children to make the scariest noises they can, one at a time. After each child makes a noise, lead the rest of the children in shouting, "I ain't scared!"

After each child has made a scary noise, say: **Now we'll go around the circle again, beginning with me. This time, let's share one thing that used to scare us—or maybe *still* scares us—but God is helping us become more courageous about.**

After you've gone around the circle, ask a volunteer to read aloud John 16:33. Say: **We told about lots of things that frighten us. But we can have courage, because Jesus has overcome the world. And because he lives with us, we can overcome our fears, too!**

The Lord Will Be Your Confidence!

Have the kids sit in a circle. Ask:
● **When have you had to be courageous?**
Read Proverbs 3:25-26. Ask:
● **What do these verses tell us about courage?**
Say: **There are many times in our lives when we need some extra courage. God wants us to trust that he'll be the confidence we need.**

Give each child a strip of paper and a pencil. Have everyone write down a situation that calls for courage. Examples might include sticking up for people who are being picked on, speaking up when something is wrong, and telling others about our faith.

When the kids are finished, fold the strips and put them in a basket.

Have each child pick a partner. Let the pair draw out one of the strips. Give pairs about five minutes to plan how they will act out their situations. Let them share their skits.

Ask the kids if they have some strategies they use when they are afraid. Remind them that they can always talk to God about their fears. Close with this prayer: **Dear God, give us courage—courage to take chances and not be afraid of making mistakes, courage to stand up for what we believe, and courage to share the good news of Jesus. In his name we pray, amen.**

The Ultimate Weapon Kit

Have the kids sit in a circle. Read Matthew 4:1-11 aloud. Ask:
- **Do you think Jesus showed courage in this story? Why?**
- **What was Jesus' defense in this conflict with the devil?**

Have children make Ultimate Weapon Kits. Give each child a small manila envelope, a ribbon that is about one and a half times the measurement of his or her waist, and several index cards. Have kids each choose a Bible passage to write on each card. They may have favorites, or you may suggest several inspiring passages. Examples might include Psalm 62:8; Proverbs 3:5-6; and John 3:16.

Have kids put the passages in their envelopes with some blank cards. Have them close the clasps of the envelopes and thread the ribbons under the flaps. Have kids tie the envelopes around their waists. Encourage the kids to keep their Ultimate Weapon Kits and to read the passages whenever they need a little courage and *encouragement* that God is on their side! Ask:
- **When are some times your Ultimate Weapon Kit might come in handy for you?**

Close in prayer, asking God to help kids to take advantage of the power of his Word to give them courage in difficult situations.

Facing Obstacles

Before class, set up an obstacle course in the room. Be sure the course is safe, challenging, and full of variety. When children arrive, encourage them to complete the obstacle course one at a time.

When everyone has completed the obstacle course, ask:
- **What did you think of this obstacle course?**

● What was the hardest part for you?

● What are some obstacles you face in your everyday life?

Read Joshua 1:9 aloud, and ask:

● What does this verse say about the way God wants you to face life's obstacles?

● How can God's presence give you courage?

Walking the Plank

Provide two lightweight narrow boards (such as crown molding) that won't reach all the way across the room when placed end to end. Be sure all the kids will fit on one board. If you have too many children to fit on one board, form more than one group to play this game and have the groups take turns.

Have all the children stand on one board. Show them how the person at the end of the line can pick up the second board and pass it down the line. The person at the other end can lay the board on the floor in front of the group. Kids must be careful that no one falls off the board they're standing on, and they'll need to help each other step onto the second board without falling off. The group must repeat this process until all of the kids have safely crossed the room.

When the game is over, ask:

● What did you notice during this game?

● How did the other people help you complete the game?

Read Acts 20:22-24 aloud and then give the children a short explanation of who Paul was and the risks he took for the sake of the gospel. Ask:

● How was Paul's mission like the game you just played?

● How can we help each other to follow God's will with courage?

Solid as a Rock

Before class, collect rocks of various sizes and clean them if necessary. Be sure you have at least a few rocks that are large and heavy, or do this activity outside if you have access to some immobile rocks. When the children arrive, encourage them to play with the rocks you have provided. You may want to encourage children to test themselves to see how strong they are, to try to break the rocks, or to build with the rocks.

After everyone has had a chance to play with the rocks, ask:

● What did you discover about these rocks?

Read Psalm 18:2-3 aloud. Then ask:

● **How do you think God is like a rock? How is he different?**

● **How do you feel when you think about God as being stronger than the biggest rock in the world?**

● **What does God's strength have to do with courage?**

● **How can you show courage to others?**

Mission: Impossible

Before class, put about a tablespoon of baking soda into a small uninflated balloon and fill a twelve-ounce plastic soda bottle about one-quarter full of vinegar.

When children have arrived, ask for a volunteer to read Exodus 1:15-21 aloud. Then ask:

● **How do you think the nurses felt about the king?**

● **Why do you think the nurses decided to disobey the king?**

● **How do you think God helped the nurses?**

Say: **The nurses wanted to obey God. Just as God gave them courage to do what was right, he can give you the courage to do what is right—even in what seem like impossible situations.**

Hold up the balloon, and say: **I'm going to do something that seems impossible. I'm going to blow up this balloon without using my mouth or your mouths or anyone else's mouth.**

Gather children around, and stretch the neck of the balloon over the neck of the bottle so the baking soda falls into the vinegar. The balloon will slowly begin to inflate. Ask:

● What did you think when I told you I could blow up this balloon without my mouth?

● What are some things you have to do that seem almost impossible?

Say: **Just as I was able to blow up the balloon with the help of some special ingredients, we're able to do what seems impossible with help from God.**

Nothing to Fear

Give each child a balloon. Help kids blow up their balloons and tie them off. Tell kids to hold their balloons in front of them and to *prepare* to squeeze the balloons until they pop. Tell them not to begin until you tell them to. Ask:

● **Why would a person feel tense or even a little afraid to pop a balloon with his or her hands?**

Remind kids to wait before they pop their balloons. Read Hebrews 13:6 aloud to the group. Ask:

● **What kinds of things are you afraid of?**

● **According to the verse I just read, why don't we need to be afraid?**

Direct kids to close their eyes and pop their balloons. Ask:

● **How many of you were seriously injured by popping your balloons?**

● **How is being afraid of popping a balloon like being afraid of some of the other things we discussed?**

Say: **God doesn't want us to do foolish things that might cause harm—but he also promises to protect us. Sometimes we may feel afraid, but we can trust God to help us face our fears with courage.**

Royal Rods

Give each child a straw, a sheet of aluminum foil, and two pieces of tape. Have children create Royal Rods by rolling their sheets of foil into balls and taping them to the tops of their straws.

Borrow a rod from one of the children. Have all the kids stand and face you. Say: **There once was a powerful king. If the king was pleased with a person he saw or heard, he would hold out his royal rod, which is called a scepter. If the king didn't raise his scepter, that person could be punished or even killed.**

Tell kids that they're going to play a game called Royal Rods. You will give them instructions and they should only obey when you lift the Royal Rod above your shoulder.

Give instructions to your kids such as "sit down" and "hop on one foot" while randomly raising and lowering the rod above and below your shoulder. If a child obeys your command when you haven't raised the rod, have him or her touch the tip of the rod you are holding to continue playing.

Explain that Esther was Jewish and she had been placed in the king's court by God's design. When God's people were threatened by a plot to destroy them, Esther was in a perfect position to step in to defend them by going directly to the king. Finish by reading Esther 5:1-3 aloud and explaining that Esther could've been killed by the king if he didn't hold out his scepter to her.

Have kids get in groups of four to discuss these questions:

● **Would you have wanted to play our game if you knew that making a mistake would result in being punished? Why or why not?**

● **Would you have gone to the king if you were Esther? Why or why not?**

● **When are some times you've needed to do something that took courage?**

● **Why do we sometimes need to do things we're afraid to do?**

● **How can we find the courage Esther had when we're afraid?**

Have kids take home their Royal Rods as reminders that God can give them the same courage that he gave Esther.

Chapter Two

Faithfulness

Human faithfulness can't stand on its own. It needs an object: someone or something to be faithful to.

God's faithfulness stems from his very nature; it needs no object, yet he chooses to be faithful to us! As God is faithful to us, we learn to trust him. And as we trust him, we slowly learn to act faithfully. God always honors our faithfulness and keeps extending his faithfulness to us even when we fail him. But faithfulness to others isn't always honored in the same way. We can remain faithful in a challenging situation because God is faithful—not because the other person deserves it, but because that's how God treats us.

These activities will help kids see lots of different aspects of faithfulness. They may associate faithfulness with other important character traits such as dependability, perseverance, and even obedience because faithfulness often requires doing things we don't feel like doing. Kids' confidence will increase as they learn that they can choose to do what's right, even if it feels uncomfortable at first. They can know that faithfulness is right, even if it's not always easy.

● ● ●

A Breath of Fresh Air

Ask each child to plug his or her nose with one hand and raise the other hand. Instruct kids to take a deep breath and hold it as long as they can. Tell children each to put their hands down after they let go of the breath. Call out the time every five seconds until all hands go down. Instruct kids to keep track of their times. Repeat the exercise three or four times, and challenge kids to beat their times each time.

Have kids get in groups of four to discuss these questions:
● Were you able to beat your own record for holding your breath?
● What did you depend on each time you stopped holding your breath?
● How would you have felt if you were unsure fresh air would be available when you needed it?

Read Romans 8:38-39 aloud, and ask:
● How is God's love as shown in these verses like the air we breathe?
● What things can get in the way of your love for God?
● What can get in the way of God's love for you?
● In our breath-holding activity, what prevented you from getting air?

Say: **The air was still there, even though you chose not to breathe it. God's love is the same way. It doesn't go away because we choose not to use it in our lives. Because God is faithful, we can depend on his love being available to us whenever we need it.** Ask:
● How does God's promise to always be there for you make you feel?

Faithfulness Prayer

Read Psalm 89:8 aloud. Ask:
● What do you think "your faithfulness surrounds you" means?
● What is faithfulness?
● What are some ways God shows faithfulness to us?

As children call out ideas, list them on a piece of newsprint or a chalkboard. Then assign each idea to a child or a group of children. Help kids come up with actions to accompany their ideas. For example, if kids say, "God makes the sun come up every morning," the assigned child or children may want to raise their arms over their heads to form circles.

When kids know what their assigned words and actions are, tell them you'll pray, thanking God for his faithfulness. When you point to a child or a group of children, they'll add their assigned ideas to the prayer and complete the actions they've planned.

Pray: **Dear God, we thank you for your faithfulness. You show us every day how much you love us, and we know we can always depend on you. We want to be faithful to you, too. Thank you for the way you show your faithfulness to us by...** (Point to one child or group at a time, giving each a chance to describe and display a way God shows his faithfulness.)

The Harvest

Before the meeting, get four different types of plant or flower seed packets.

Give each child four sheets of paper, four pieces of transparent tape, and four different types of seeds. Have kids tape each of their seeds to a different sheet of paper. Have kids form groups of four, and set out markers.

Ask groups to decide what kind of plant each seed will grow into. Then have kids draw the mature plant next to each seed.

Say: **Please listen as I tell you a story about seeds.** Read Matthew 13:31-32 aloud. Tell the kids what each one of their seeds will grow into. Then ask:

● **How much bigger will the plants be than the seeds you have?**
● **What will the seeds need in order to grow?**
● **What kinds of things make our faith grow?**

Say: **We've all been given little seeds of faith. When we pray, read our Bibles, worship God, and serve others, our faith grows. If we faithfully take care of what God plants in our lives, our faith will grow much bigger—just like the little seeds will grow bigger when you plant them. Write or draw one thing that will help your faith grow on each of your papers. Then take your seeds home and plant them. As you do the things that will help the plants grow, remember to do the things that will help your faith grow, too.**

Faithful Followers

Set up a trail for an imaginary journey in your room. First lay down a straight line of masking tape, about three feet long. At the end of the line, place a stack of paper. Leave a three-foot space and then set up two chairs about a foot apart. Finally, set up a table for children to crawl under. Place a sheet over the table.

Prepare a snack of trail mix to share at the end of the journey.

Have children form a line at the start of the trail. Say: **You are about to begin a journey that ends with a sweet reward. You may face danger.**

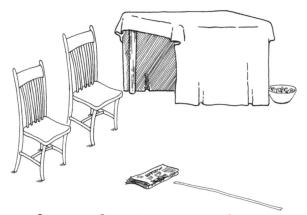

If you turn away from my directions, you may become a sweet reward for the beasts on the trail, so do everything exactly as I tell you.

Demonstrate the following directions:

Walk on the masking tape "bridge" to the pile of newspaper "rocks." Place a rock in the middle of the open space and step on it to get over the "crocodile-infested river." Then walk around the "sand pit" chairs in a figure-eight pattern to avoid sinking. To finish, crawl through the table "cave" and pick up some trail mix at the end.

After every child has completed the trail, ask:

● **If this had been a real trail and you came upon all those dangers, how important would it have been to follow each direction carefully?**

Say: **The Bible tells about an eight-year-old king named Josiah. He was young, like you, and he was beginning the dangerous journey of leading his people.** Have someone read aloud 2 Chronicles 34:1-3. Then ask:

● **Why do you think Josiah sought God and followed his directions?**

● **What does Josiah's example show us?**

Say: **Josiah was faithful to do what was right in the sight of the Lord, just as you were faithful to the directions I gave you on our imaginary trail. Being faithful means not only knowing the right thing to do but also following through with it.** Ask:

● **What are some things you need to be faithful about this week?**

You're My Hero

Set miscellaneous costume items—including funny hats, construction paper, and markers—in a pile. Have children form groups of five. In each group, have children dress up a group member as a super hero and create a super-hero slogan—for example, a group might use "Man of Steel" as a slogan. After five minutes, have groups present their super heroes to the class. Applaud each group's efforts and then ask:

● **What qualities does a good super-hero have?**

● **What real-life heroes do you know? What makes them heroes?**

Ask a volunteer to read aloud Hebrews 11:1-2, 23-27. Then say: **People who show faith in God help us to know God better. We could call these people "faith heroes." The book of Hebrews talks about faith heroes such as Noah, who built the ark because God told him to; Abraham, who trusted God enough to live in a new country; and Moses, who stood up to a bad king even though he was afraid.** Ask:

● **How did these heroes show their faith in God?**

● **What qualities did these heroes have?**

● **Do you know people today who show their faith? Explain.**

Have children get into groups of five again to create new heroes—faith heroes—with new slogans. After five minutes, have groups present their heroes. Ask:

● **How can faith heroes help us to be faithful?**

● **How can you be a faith hero this week?**

In Noah's Faithful Shoes

You'll need a big pair of shoes or sandals for this activity.

Say: **You know what? God sometimes asks people to do things they don't fully understand—things that may seem strange at the time! Let's read about something God asked one of his people to do.**

Read Genesis 6:6-17 aloud. Then say: **It had never rained when God had Noah start building the ark. The ark was over a football field long. It took around one hundred years for Noah and his sons to build the ark. Do any of those things sound strange to you?**

Place the shoes in the center of the room, and have kids circle around them. Say: **Put yourself in Noah's shoes and think about what must have happened as this huge boat began to take shape on his property. I'm going to ask a few questions. When you have an answer to a question, go and stand in "Noah's shoes" and give your answer.**

Ask the following questions, allowing a few children to stand in Noah's shoes one at a time to give answers to each question.

● What do you think Noah's neighbors might have thought?

● What do you think they might have said to Noah?

● What might you have said to Noah if you lived back then and didn't follow God?

● How would you have felt if you were Noah?

● What are some things God asks people to do today that might make others say, "You're crazy for doing that!"?

Say: **Noah probably got discouraged sometimes. But did he give up? Let's see what the Bible says.** Read aloud Genesis 6:22. Say: **Noah was faithful to God. He did what God told him to do.** Ask:

● When are some times you've gotten discouraged while trying to do what was right?

● What do you think Noah might say to kids today about being faithful?

Have kids stand in the shoes again as they answer.

True-Blue Clues

Set up a clue hunt in your church building or around your church grounds. Write clues that describe specific locations. Place the clues where kids will find each one and be led to the next clue. For example, to start the hunt, you might give a group the clue, "Look in the place where the Good News is preached." Place the second clue where your minister stands to preach. Place at least four or five different clues. The last clue should lead kids back to your meeting place.

When kids arrive, form groups of about four. Give each group the first clue, but allow about a minute between groups' departures. Tell kids to leave the clues they find where they are so the next group can see them.

When all the groups have returned, ask:

● How did you find your way back here?

● Would you have found your way back if you hadn't followed every clue? Why or why not?

Have someone read aloud Genesis 12:1-9. Ask:

● How is what we did similar to what Abram did?

● What clues was Abram following?

● How was Abram faithful to God?

● How can we be faithful in following God?

Say: **Abram followed God faithfully even when he didn't know** where God was leading him. We can follow God faithfully one step at a time, just as you did in the game we played.

● Where do we get the "clues" that teach us how to follow God faithfully?

● How can you follow God today?

God First

Say: **God wants us to obey our parents and people who have authority over us, such as teachers and our government. But when someone wants us to do something that goes against God's laws, we need to obey God rather than people. Let's look at a story in the Bible in which that happened.**

Form groups of about four, and read aloud Acts 5:17-29. Then have groups each write a short song to sing to a familiar tune that tells the message of this passage. You may want to sing the following as a sample, or you could just have kids sing this song a few times before moving on to the questions.

We Obey Jesus
(sung to the tune of "Jesus Loves Me")

> **Jesus' disciples went to jail**
> **For telling of Jesus without fail.**
> **An angel set them free that night**
> **To teach again at morning's light.**
> **We obey Jesus,**
> **We obey Jesus,**
> **We obey Jesus**
> **And tell about his love.**

After kids have written and presented their songs, ask:

● **What was tough about the apostles' decision to keep preaching about Jesus?**

● **What helped them to be faithful to God?**

● **What does it mean for us to be faithful to God?**

● **How does God help us to be faithful to him?**

Sing the sample song or kids' songs again to wrap up the activity.

Wake Up

Have kids get into pairs. Have kids in each pair tell their partners what their morning routines are like. Then have each pair pantomime for the rest of the group what it looks like when they try to wake up in the morning. Give examples of things that might happen, such as a parent knocking on the door a dozen times or the child hitting the snooze button on his or her alarm clock or throwing covers over his or her head. After each pair has had a chance to pantomime, gather everyone in a circle. Ask:

● **How does it feel when someone or something wakes you up from a deep sleep?**

● **Why is it harder to wake up some days than others?**

● **Why is it important to get up each morning, even if we don't feel like it?**

Read aloud Luke 9:23. Say: **When the Bible says to take up our cross daily, it means we choose to follow God every day, just as we choose to get out of bed every day.** Ask:

● **Why is it important for us to choose to follow God every day?**

● **What kinds of days might make it hard to follow God?**

● **When might you not really feel like following God?**

Say: **Even though it's really hard sometimes to get up in the morning, we do it. We know we have to go to school, go to practice, or keep an appointment. That's what faithfulness is—following through with what we know is right even if we don't feel like it. Just as we faithfully get up each day, we need to choose to follow God each day. When we do, we are being faithful to him.**

Leap of Faith!

Have kids sit in a circle. Ask:

● **What is one thing you believe to be true?**

Have each child think about one thing they believe to be true (for example, someone's belief might be, "I believe I was born on November 24, 1987.") Say: **Let's find out how faithful you are to that belief. Jump up, count to five, and sit back down after each of the following questions if your answer is "yes."** Ask:

● **Would you be willing to tell others about this belief?**

● **Would you be willing to go to prison for this belief?**

● Would you be willing to die for this belief?

Say: **The Bible tells us of a man named Paul who was truly faithful to his belief in Jesus. To be faithful means you are loyal and not willing to give up. Paul was faithful to Jesus even when Paul was put in prison and threatened with death.**

Read Philippians 1:12-14 and 4:10-13 aloud.

Say: **Being faithful is not easy! We're going to play a game that will help us share some ideas about how we can stay faithful to Jesus even when it's tough.**

Put a plate of treats across the room or at the end of a hallway. Have the kids stand in a line facing the treats. Play Leap Frog down the hall to reach the goal. Each time a child leaps over another person to get to the front of the line, he or she must offer one tip that will help Christians stay faithful. Examples might include:

● Read the Bible
● Attend church and Sunday school
● Tell others the Good News of Jesus
● Seek out other Christian friends

You may wish to write down their suggestions. After everyone offers a tip, enjoy the treats together and discuss kids' terrific suggestions for staying faithful.

Talent, Cubed!

Summarize the story of Samson, who was chosen by God for special service before he was even born and given the gift of incredible physical strength. Samson did great things for God, but he also misused his gift with selfish motives and he eventually was separated from God through his wrong choices. Read Judges 16:28-30 aloud.

Say: **Samson was given a special talent by God: great strength. Samson didn't always act faithfully, but God always did! God was faithful when Samson finally called upon him for help.** Ask:

● **Where do our talents come from?**
● **What are some of your talents?**
● **How can we use these talents to be faithful to God?**

Make a Talent Cube. Give each child a copy of the Talent Cube. (Make one photocopy of the pattern on page 25 on tagboard for each child before class.) Have each child write or draw six things that he or she is good

24

at, one in each square. Then have the children cut out the cubes, fold them, and tape the edges.

Have each child be seated with a partner. The pairs will take turns rolling their cubes and then describing how the talent shown on the cube can be used to be faithful to God. For example, if someone is good at singing, he or she could sing at a nursing home to brighten people's lives. If someone is good at football, he or she could be a positive leader on a team and a good example of sportsmanship. If someone is good at coloring, he or she could make pictures for people who are sick to make them smile.

Say: **All of our talents come from God. We can use them faithfully to honor God.**

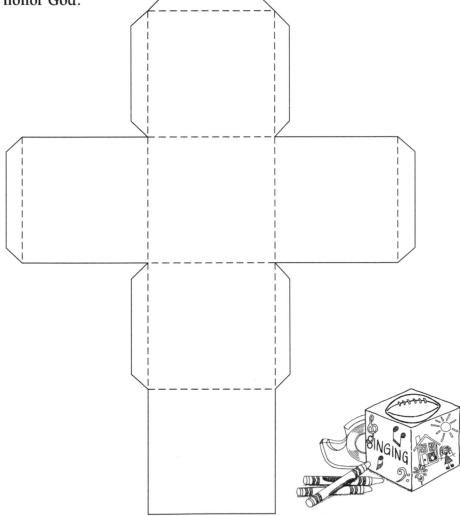

Chapter Three

Forgiveness

Unforgiveness has changed the world our kids will inherit into a place of growing gang violence, unpredictable road rage, and lawsuits that will cost them billions of dollars in insurance premiums. People who cannot forgive are compelled to seek revenge and assign blame when answers don't satisfy. When turned inward, that same need for revenge becomes destructive guilt and self-hatred.

Forgiveness frees us from that vicious natural cycle. Practicing forgiveness doesn't make kids doormats. It empowers them! When kids choose to live in forgiveness, they're no longer driven by forces of anger and hurt. We can allow God to help us face a bad situation and to handle it in a way that pleases him. Forgiveness opens the door to mercy, peace, and a better world to live in.

Kids *can* choose to forgive and to be forgiven. The activities in this section will help them see how God forgives us through Jesus and requires that we forgive others in the same way, with his help.

● ● ●

Tied Up in Knots

Have kids stand in a tight circle. Direct them to form a human knot by each holding the hands of two different people across the circle. Make sure that each of the children is holding two hands. Tell them that one hand represents anger and the other hand represents hurt. Instruct kids to attempt to get out of the human knot *without* letting go of each other's hands.

After about two minutes, have kids freeze while you read

Matthew 6:14-15 aloud. While kids are still in the human knot, have them discuss the following questions:

- **How is this human knot like unforgiveness?**
- **What happens to a relationship when the people involved hold on to their anger or hurt?**

Say: **There's a simple way to get out of this knot of unforgiveness. Got any ideas?** Have the kids let go of each others' hands. Ask:

- **What did this human knot show you that we have to do in order to forgive?**
- **Why do you think it's so important to God that we forgive each other?**
- **What does forgiveness do for a relationship?**

Remind kids that God has forgiven us and that we need to follow his example. Have kids take a minute to think about people they may need to forgive. Encourage kids to apologize to God for not forgiving and to ask him to help them forgive the people who have wronged them.

Foiled Again

Have kids get in groups of three. Give each child a small sheet of aluminum foil. Encourage kids to share with the group about the forgiveness of a sin. Direct children to crumple up their sheets of foil as they share or think about their sins. Read Ephesians 2:1-5 aloud, and have groups discuss these questions:

- **What does sin do to our lives?**
- **How is the crumpled foil like sin?**
- **If we're dead in our sins, how can we become alive again?**

Read verse 5 aloud again.

Instruct students to uncrumple their sheets of foil and make them as flat as possible. Ask:

- **Were you able to make your sheet of foil look brand-new again? Why or why not?**

Ask a volunteer to read 2 Corinthians 5:17 aloud. While the volunteer is reading, give each child a new sheet of foil. Have trios discuss these questions:

- **How is the new sheet of foil like what Jesus has done for us?**
- **Why is it important to ask Jesus to forgive our sins?**

Remind kids that when they ask Jesus to forgive their sins, he makes them brand-new again. In closing, give kids some quiet time to pray individually about anything this lesson has reminded them about.

Cleaning Up

Have children perform this skit and then discuss its meaning.

Scene: Children are walking through the halls at school.

Props: The Wrongdoer should use face paints to create green smudges on his or her face and arms. Three Forgivers should each have a slightly damp washcloth. Children should carry books or backpacks as they would at school.

Script

Voice from offstage: "Bear with each other and forgive whatever grievances you may have against one another. Forgive as the Lord forgave you" (Colossians 3:13).
(Wrongdoer enters and stands center stage.)

Wrongdoer: I feel really terrible. I blew up at some of my friends. I'm afraid to talk to them, but I can't stand this feeling anymore.
(Three Forgivers enter, and Wrongdoer stands center stage with his or her back to the audience. Forgivers stand, facing the audience and the Wrongdoer, so each can be seen.)

Wrongdoer: *(Nervously, to first Forgiver)* Hi. I blew up at you because I was upset about a bad grade. I'm really sorry. Will you forgive me?

First Forgiver: I sure understand how a bad grade can make you feel. Yes, I forgive you.
(First Forgiver uses a damp towel to wipe a smudge off of Wrongdoer's face or arms.)

Wrongdoer: *(To second Forgiver)* I'm sorry I was jealous that you'd done so well on the test. Will you forgive me?

Second Forgiver: You're my friend. Of course I forgive you.
(Second Forgiver uses a damp towel to wipe a smudge off of Wrongdoer's face or arms.)

Wrongdoer: *(To third Forgiver)* I lied to you about the test because I didn't want you to think I was stupid. I'm really sorry. Can you forgive me?

Third Forgiver: Sure, I forgive you. You don't have to lie to me. I know you're not stupid.

(Third Forgiver uses a damp towel to wipe a smudge off of Wrongdoer's face or arms.)

Wrongdoer: *(Facing audience)* Wow, I feel a lot better now...cleaner somehow.
(Wrongdoer joins the Forgivers and then all the children hurry offstage as if a bell has rung.)

Pause as the presenters rejoin the group. Ask:
● **What important things happened in this skit?**
● **When are you like the Wrongdoer? Like the Forgivers?**
● **Why is it important to forgive?**
● **How can we forgive people who have really hurt us?**
● **We don't use washcloths to show forgiveness. What are some ways we can show that we forgive?**

Keep on Forgiving

Form groups of about four. Give each group a stack of building blocks, and tell groups to build the tallest structures they can. Secretly ask one member of each group to knock the group's structure over each time it is nearly completed. Encourage kids to rebuild each time the structure is destroyed. Allow enough time for each group to repeat the process several times. When you have groups stop building, ask:
● **How did you feel when your building got knocked down?**
● **Did you feel like forgiving? Why or why not?**
Say: **Let's take a look at someone in the Bible who wasn't sure about forgiving someone lots of times.** Read aloud Matthew 18:21-22. Ask:
● **Do you think Peter felt like forgiving that many times?**
● **Why do you think Jesus said what he did?**
Say: **I asked one member of each group to knock down your buildings many times. I did it to help you see that it's sometimes hard to forgive people. Please forgive your group member.** Ask:
● **Who do you have trouble forgiving? Why?**
Say: **God will help us forgive when we don't want to or when the situation seems too bad to forgive. Let's ask God to help us forgive others for the times they treat us badly.**

Pray together, asking God to help your kids forgive others as he wants them to forgive.

Cleansing Forgiveness

Prepare a table by protecting it with plastic, such as a garbage bag. You'll need a clear container that will hold at least four cups of liquid, a package of grape-flavored powdered drink mix in a small plastic bag, a spoon, and a cup of bleach. Pour about one cup of water into the container.

Say: **God wants our lives to be clear of sin, just like this water is clear and clean. But the Bible tells us that we've all sinned and fallen short of God's glory. When we sin, our relationship with God is changed, just like this powder changes the water.**

Take a pinch of the drink mix and drop it into the water. Say: **Now I want you to think for a minute about something you've done that you know was displeasing to God. When you think of something, come take a pinch of this powder and drop it into the water.** (If you have more than ten children, you might want to use multiple containers.)

When kids have each put their pinch of drink mix in the water, hold up the container to show how "dirty" the water is. Say: **Sin keeps us from having a relationship with God. And there's nothing we can do about sin in our lives on our own. But thankfully, God has a plan and he is willing to forgive us.** Have someone read aloud 1 John 1:9. Ask:
- **What do we need to do in order to be forgiven?**
- **What does it mean to confess our sins?**
- **What does God promise to do?**

Say: **When we confess our sins and ask for forgiveness, God cleanses our lives of sin.** Pour a cup of bleach into the container, and stir it with a spoon. In a few seconds, the water will turn clear.

Say: **Think silently about things you might need to ask God to forgive you for. Then confess your sin to him, and ask him to forgive you.**

If you feel it's appropriate, this would be a good time to explain God's plan of redemption more fully.

Tough to Forgive

Gather enough egg-sized stones for children to each have one. You'll also need fine-tipped watercolor markers, a pail half-full of soapy water, and paper towels.

Say: **Sometimes it's tough to forgive someone who's done something bad to us, but that's what God wants us to do. We're going to** take a look at someone in the Bible who forgave people when they were really doing something bad to him. Stephen had just told the people about who Jesus was and that they had killed him on the cross. Let's see what the people's response was.

Read aloud Acts 7:54-58. Then ask:

● **If you were Stephen, how would you feel toward the people with the stones?**

● **How do you think Stephen responded?**

Read aloud Acts 7:59-60. Then ask:

● **How do you think Stephen was able to respond the way he did?**

Distribute stones to kids, but caution them to hold on to the stones. Then say: **Think right now about the worst thing someone has ever done to you, and write or draw it on your stone. No one will be reading your stone but you.** After kids have written on their stones, say: **Now ask God to help you forgive that person. If you're willing to forgive that person, come up and wash the words or picture off of your stone.**

Allow kids a few minutes to think and to wash their stones in the pail of water. Then say: **Now you can take your stone home as a reminder of how Stephen forgave the people who were stoning him to death and how you can forgive others who hurt you.**

Be Like God

Have children get into groups of four to six, and provide three props for each group. For example, one group might receive a pack of cotton balls, a backpack, and a toothbrush, while another group receives a candy bar, a schoolbook, and a flashlight. Explain to the kids that they must create a skit using their props. The only rules are:

● they must use all three props in some way,

● each person in the group must be involved in the skit, and

● the skit must show someone being forgiven.

List these three rules on a chalkboard or easel as a reminder. Encourage humor and creativity, and reassure shy kids by letting them know that even though every person must be in the skit, not everyone must necessarily speak. For example, Tony could be a tree or a door in his group's skit.

Allow several minutes for groups to create their skits and then gather everyone together. Explain that each group will now perform its skit.

Have the audience watch for the person being forgiven. Pause after each group performs its skit, and ask:

- **Why did** (name) **need forgiveness in this skit?**
- **How was** (name) **forgiven?**

After all skits have been performed, congratulate kids on a job well-done. Then ask:

- **How does it feel when someone forgives you? When someone refuses to forgive you?**
- **How does it feel to forgive someone else?**
- **Why is it important to forgive?**

Read aloud Ephesians 4:32 and Colossians 3:13. Say: **When we decide to follow Jesus and confess our sins, God forgives us completely for everything we've done wrong. He wants us to be like him. He teaches us about forgiveness by forgiving us. Then we can ask him to help us forgive others.**

What's Fair?

Ask children to form pairs.

Say: **Let me tell you three stories. In each story, someone destroys something. I want you to decide who should pay in each story...and how much should be paid.**

After each story, ask children to discuss this question in their pairs:

- **Who should pay? How much?**

When children have had adequate time to reach conclusions, ask pairs to share what they decided.

Story 1—Shawn Gabriel parked his new eighteen-speed racing bike outside a store. He locked his bike with a chain, but he discovered when he came back that a boy was smashing the bike with a metal rod. A man ran up and stopped the boy who was hitting the bike, but already the bike's spokes were broken, the paint was scratched, and the frame was bent. The bike was a mess. The boy who did the damage was caught.

Story 2—When Adrienne Lynn got to school last Monday, all the other girls were laughing at her. Even Adrienne's best friend, Sheila, was snickering. Adrienne found out later that a girl named Michelle had told lies about her—and now everyone believed that Adrienne did some terrible things. Adrienne's reputation is destroyed.

Story 3—Jesus didn't do anything wrong, but he was arrested. Then he was beaten. Then he was nailed to a cross and murdered. Jesus did this because someone sinned and the only way to save the sinner was to die in the sinner's place. The Bible says in Romans 3:23-24 that both you and I are sinners, so Jesus died in our place.

Say: **Someone destroys a bike, damages a reputation, or takes a life. And the person who did it has to pay. That's justice. It's fair.**

But forgiveness happens when the person who was hurt decides to pay. If you break my window and I make you pay, that's justice. If I pay for it myself and let you off, that's forgiveness. Or if there's no way you can pay and I don't hold it against you, that's forgiveness.

Have kids discuss these questions:

● When is a time somebody else paid for something you did wrong?

● How did it feel to be forgiven?

● Have you ever forgiven another person?

● How did it feel to forgive another person?

Forgiveness: Caught, Not Taught

The best way for someone to learn forgiveness is to be forgiven. The second-best way is for that person to see forgiveness in action—to see it modeled.

Gather your children around you, and share one time that you've been forgiven for something you did or a time you've forgiven another person. Your story can be particularly effective if you can relate something that happened to you as a child.

Follow up your story with these questions:

● What was forgiven?

● Who did the forgiving?

● Have you ever been forgiven?

● Who forgave you? How did that feel?

● When have you forgiven someone else?

Distribute two chenille wires to each child. Say: **You've had someone forgive you. Jesus died on a cross for you. Listen to this passage.** Read John 3:16 aloud. Ask children to each create a cross using their chenille wires as they discuss these questions:

● Why did Jesus die for us?

● How do you feel, knowing Jesus died for you?

● How does the knowledge of Jesus' forgiveness affect your choice to forgive others?

Smash Bash!

Have the kids sit in a circle. Ask:

● **When has someone done something to you that made you very, very mad?**

● **How did you feel about forgiving that person?**

Say: **To forgive means to choose to stop being resentful or mad at a person who did something mean to you and to give up your desire to get back at the person.** Ask:

● **Has anyone ever done something to you that has been impossible for you to forgive?**

Read aloud Colossians 2:13-14 and 3:8.

Say: **God has already forgiven you because of Christ's sacrifice! This allows you to forgive others—to put aside your anger, rage, and malice (bad feelings) toward someone else— because that is what Christ did for you.**

Give each child a piece of clay. Ask kids to each create something with the clay that reminds them of something they haven't yet forgiven. When the creations are done, have each person show and explain his or her creation to one other person.

Have kids stand in a circle with their creations. Say this prayer: **Dear God, sometimes it's hard to forgive other people. As we "smash" our sadness, our resentment, and our disappointment, please help us to forgive just as you have forgiven us. In Jesus' name, amen.**

One at a time, have kids smash the clay creations. Have the kids each reshape their clay into something that reminds them of forgiveness. Then have them share their new creations with the whole group.

Extra-Step Snack Stash Story

Set up a table with several bowls on it. Fill the bowls with snacks that represent the gifts that Joseph gave to his brothers. Examples of snacks are circle-shaped cereal to represent cart tires, fish-shaped crackers to represent food, fruit-leather pieces to represent clothes, and M&Ms to represent money. Have the kids sit in a row on the floor in front of the table. Stand in front of the table, and ask:

● **When someone hits you on purpose, what is your first reaction?**

● Now, if someone tried to kill you, would you be likely to forgive him or her and then give him or her lots of presents? ("No way!" is the likely response.)

Say: **I'm going to tell you about a man named Joseph who did just that. This is a remarkable story of forgiveness and taking the extra step to bless those who are mean to you.**

Joseph had many brothers. His brothers were jealous of him, so they sold him to be a slave. Joseph was taken to Egypt, where he became a very important and powerful person. Many years later there was a great famine, which means that there was nothing to eat. God had warned Joseph about the famine, so Egypt had been saving food. Joseph's brothers came to Egypt to look for food, and although they didn't know it, they spoke directly to Joseph, the brother whom they had sold years ago.

Give each child a paper cup. Read the end of the story in Genesis 45:1-24. As you read about the gifts that Joseph gave to his brothers, have the kids stand up in a line and file past the snack table, scooping into their cups the gifts that Joseph gave to his brothers.

While the kids snack, ask:

● **How do you think Joseph felt when he first saw his brothers?**

● **Tell me about a situation in which you could forgive someone and take the extra step to bless him or her.**

Say: **Joseph not only forgave his brothers—he saved their lives! He forgave them for what they had done to him, and he took the extra step of providing for them. Remember Joseph's example, because God was very pleased with him.**

Chapter Four

Honesty

Honesty is the starting point for so many important things! People who resist being honest with themselves miss out on confession that leads to forgiveness. People who can't be honest with others miss out on dependability that leads to trust, on honor that leads to integrity, and on sincerity that builds strong relationships.

Deception began in the Garden of Eden and is relearned by each generation. Kids find out early that if they can cover up a wrong choice, they can sometimes avoid punishment. If they blame someone else, they might not look so bad. Even though dishonesty is often a reaction to fear, it creates a whole new fear: the fear of being found out. God wants to give us freedom from all our fear in his perfect love (1 John 4:18). Kids can become honest as they learn that God demands honesty from us out of his love, not out of a desire to see us punished.

These activities will help kids see honesty as a choice that benefits both themselves and others and, while honesty may be painful for a moment, it is best in the long run.

● ● ●

True Colors

Fill an ice-cube tray with water that has been heavily colored with food coloring. Freeze the ice cubes before you meet with your children.

Gather your children around you as you fill a large, clear glass full of warm water. Suggest the glass of clean, clear water represents their lives.

Show children several of the colored ice cubes. Say: **Let's say these** small ice cubes are lies you tell. See what happens when we mix these lies into our lives.

Drop the ice cubes in the warm water. They'll immediately begin to melt—and their color will soon tinge all the water in the glass. To speed up the process, stir the cubes with a spoon or a straw.

Discuss these questions:
- What did you see happen?
- Why did it happen?
- How might this be like telling lies?

Say: It didn't take many ice cubes to contaminate all the water. Just a few changed the color of the entire glass! That's what it's like trying to be honest in just one part of your life while you're being dishonest in other areas. Even a few lies change a person's entire character.

Ask a student to read aloud James 3:9-11. Ask:
- What does this passage say about being honest?
- Can we be honest and dishonest at the same time?

Say: Just as the ice cube colored the whole glass of water, lies color our whole lives. Honest words and actions help us keep a clear conscience.

Public Lies, Private Eyes

Have kids get in groups of three. Tell the children that they're going to be detectives. Explain that you're going to tell three stories, and each group can ask one question about each story to try to discover which one of the three stories isn't true. Give each group a sheet of paper and a pencil to take down notes and write down their questions. Tell three stories about things that happened to you. Make sure two of them are true and one is false but possible.

After your first story, let groups each decide on the one question to ask that will help them learn whether the story is true or not. Do the same thing with the second and third stories. Then give each group a minute to decide which story is untrue. Allow each group to make a guess. After all the groups have guessed, reveal which story was untrue.

Then have groups discuss these questions:
- How did you come up with your guess about which story was untrue?
- Is it hard to fool people by telling them things that aren't true?

Why or why not?
- **Do you think God is sometimes fooled when we say things that aren't true? Why or why not?**
- **Read Ephesians 4:25. Why do you think God wants us to avoid telling lies?**

In their groups, have kids tell each other at least three reasons it's important to tell the truth.

Scrambled Choices

Before this activity, use masking tape to create four sections on your meeting-room floor that are each large enough for all your kids to stand in. Number the sections from one to four.

Tell kids that you're going to give them different situations and a list of responses for each situation. Explain that kids should move to the section that matches the response they would probably give to each situation.

Situation 1—Your three best friends are talking about a television show they watched last night. All three of them think the show was really funny, but your parents didn't let you watch it because of the bad language the characters sometimes use. One of your friends asks you what you thought of the show. You'd say:
- Response 1—"I thought the show was pretty funny."
- Response 2—"I missed the show last night."
- Response 3—"I don't watch that show."
- Response 4—"My parents don't let me watch that show."

Situation 2—While playing at your grandparents' house, you accidentally knock over a collectors plate that your grandparents say is worth two hundred dollars. The plate isn't too badly broken, and you're certain you can fix it if your grandparents would let you use their super glue. What would you do?
- Response 1—Hide the plate under the bed.
- Response 2—Ask your grandparents if you can borrow their super glue to fix a toy.
- Response 3—Ask your grandparents if you can borrow their super glue to fix something you broke.
- Response 4—Tell your grandparents you broke their plate.

After each situation, have a representative from each section explain why he or she went to that section. Try to summarize the reasons for lying and the reasons for telling the truth that your kids gave. Then read Matthew 27:11-14 aloud. Explain to the children that Jesus probably would have been released if he had lied to Pilate. Then ask:

● **Why did Jesus choose to tell the truth to Pilate when he could have lied and been set free?**

● **How do you think Jesus might have reacted in the situations we discussed?**

● **Would you change any of your responses to the situations based on Jesus' example? Explain.**

● **How do you think you might behave differently the next time you're faced with something that you could lie about?**

Fortune Fibs

Bring in a box of fortune cookies (available at most grocery stores). Give each child a cookie, and have children take turns reading aloud their fortunes. While children are munching their cookies, ask:

● **What's your reaction to your fortune?**

● **Do you want to believe that your fortune will come true? Why or why not?**

Have a volunteer read aloud Proverbs 12:19 and then ask:

● **When have you wanted to lie about something?**

● **Why do you think "a lying tongue lasts only a moment"?**

● **How is your fortune similar to a lie?**

● **What are some reasons God wants us to be honest?**

Say: **Sometimes lying seems like a good idea because we think it will make something seem better than it really is or not as bad as it really is. But just as our fortune cookies didn't last very long, the lies we tell don't last very long either. Honesty isn't like the fortunes in our cookies. Honesty is real and true and it lasts forever.**

To Tell the Truth

Give each child a rubber band. Have kids hold the rubber bands with both hands and stretch them tight. Then have kids each try to let go of both ends of their rubber bands at the same time. Give kids several attempts. Then collect the rubber bands, and ask:

● **Did you get snapped by the rubber band? Why?**

● Did the same hand always get snapped? Why not?

● How is stretching the rubber band and letting it go similar to telling a lie?

Read Proverbs 19:5 aloud. Then ask:

● What was the consequence of letting the rubber band go?

● What are some of the consequences of lying?

● Who gets hurt when we lie?

Say: **When we lie, we hurt ourselves, we hurt others, and we disappoint God. Our Bible verse tells us that we won't escape the consequences of our lies.** Ask:

● Is there anyone you need to apologize to who might have been hurt by a lie?

Say: **God's best for us includes developing the habit of honesty and honestly handling the times we fail.**

Peter's Problem

Gather the kids together. Ask:

● Have you ever been afraid of telling the truth, so you told a lie instead?

If kids are reluctant to answer this question, you can give an example from your own childhood or come up with a hypothetical situation. Then ask:

● How did you feel after you told the lie?

Say: **One of Jesus' followers betrayed Jesus with a lie. He did this because he was afraid, not because he was a bad or evil man.**

Explain that the passage they are going to hear tells about the night when Jesus was arrested, a very scary time for the followers of Jesus. Read or have a child read Matthew 26:69-75.

Say: **Peter was afraid that something terrible would happen to him if he admitted that he knew Jesus. That's why he lied and pretended he didn't know him. Peter was a good man who loved Jesus. He didn't set out to be dishonest. He made a bad choice because of his fear.**

Tell the kids that they will act out the story in a way that will allow them to show some alternatives Peter could have used instead of lying. Appoint someone to play Peter and someone to play each of the characters who asks Peter questions. The rest of the group will be roosters who will say "cock-a-doodle-doo" when they hear the word "crowed."

Read the story again, and each time Peter is asked a question, tell everyone to freeze. Ask:

● **What could Peter have said or done?**

Then signal for kids to unfreeze and act out what Peter actually did in the situation.

After the skit is complete, say: **Peter decided to lie because he was afraid.** Ask:

● **What does it take to choose to be honest?**

● **How can you be honest even when you are afraid?**

Say: **I'm sure Peter learned a lot about honesty from his experience, because he went on to serve Jesus for the rest of his life.**

If you have time, you might want to give your kids a chance to build a church using marshmallow "rocks" and frosting "mortar" to remind kids that Peter, the rock, was charged with building the New Testament church.

Silly Stories

Collect one prop for each child. These can be anything, but they might include an old photograph, a hat, a stuffed animal, a ball, a rolling pin, and a paintbrush. Put the props in a box or a basket.

Gather the kids together.

Say: **I've collected some fun props for you to make up sentence stories about. Make your stories as fun and silly as you like. I'll show you what I mean.**

Pick up one of the props and make up a sentence story about it, such as, "This ball was used to hit a home run in the World Series just last year."

When each child has had a chance to tell his or her story, ask:

● **How did making up the stories make you feel?**

● **It's fun and creative to make up stories, but have you ever told a story and someone thought you were telling the truth? How did you feel then?**

● **What is the difference between creating a story and telling a lie?**

Say: **The Bible tells us that lying is wrong. The Bible also talks about how good we feel when we are honest.** Read Proverbs 24:26 aloud, and say: **This verse tells us that an honest answer is like a sign of deep affection between two people. When you make up stories to entertain people or surprises that will make them happy, it gives the** same kind of message of deep affection. That is entirely different than trying to make someone believe something that isn't true. Ask:

● **What are some reasons we might want someone to believe something that isn't true?**

● **Do you think most of these reasons show more thought for self or for others?**

Say: **When we're honest, as God wants us to be, we honor both ourselves and others.**

Be Honest in Everything

Gather rulers, tape measures, and scales. Also, gather items kids can weigh and measure. Have kids form pairs or trios, and instruct them to guess how long an item is or how much it weighs. Then have kids weigh and measure the item to see how accurate their guesses were. Ask:

● **How good were you at guessing how long something is or how much something weighs?**

● **If you were buying something that had to be weighed and measured in order to see how much it cost, would you want the salesperson to guess its length or weight? Why or why not?**

Have kids form three groups, and have each group read one of the following passages: Leviticus 19:35-36; Deuteronomy 25:13-16; and Proverbs 11:1. Ask:

● **What kind of action is described in your verse and what does God say about it?**

● **What are some ways people are dishonest today?**

● **Why do you think God wants people who follow him to be honest?**

Close in prayer, asking God to help each child to always be honest.

Televised Truths

Before the activity, gather circle-shaped snack crackers and cheese in aerosol cans.

When kids have gathered, read Exodus 23:1a aloud. Ask:

● **What does this verse tell us not to do?**

● **What does it mean to give a false report?**

● **Why do you think God tells us not to tell lies about others?**

● How do you feel if someone tells a lie about you?

Say: **Even though God told people not to lie about others a long time ago, he still wants us to always tell the truth about others. Today we're going to develop a snack that reminds us to tell the truth.**

Direct kids to the crackers and cheese. Have them use the cheese to write letters on the crackers. They can work together to spell out a phrase such as "tell the truth." If you have younger children in the group, have them each write a T on a cracker to stand for truth. Have the kids use their decorated crackers as props for a television-like commercial for truth. For example, they might hold up crackers and say, "Truth: the tasty treat!" Kids can work alone or in groups. You might even want to videotape these commercials. When kids are finished with their commercials, let them enjoy the snacks together.

Ice-Cube Hideaway

Form pairs, and ask partners to sit knee-to-knee facing each other. Ask the member of each pair who's wearing the most blue to come to you and get an ice cube and then return to sit knee-to-knee with his or her partner. Ask the members of the pairs who aren't holding ice cubes to close their eyes. Then tell the partners holding ice cubes to each hide the cube in a fist and hold both fists out where their partners can see them.

Say: **Now open your eyes, partners, and see if you can tell which fist the ice cube is in. But don't choose yet! Let's wait sixty seconds and then see if you can tell.**

Count down the sixty seconds in ten-second increments and then ask for partners to each choose which hand the cube is in. The melting ice makes it very clear which hands are harboring ice cubes. Collect and dispose of the ice.

Discuss these questions:

● **Why was it so easy to find the ice cubes?**

● **How did it feel when you tried to hide ice cubes from view?**

Say: **Sometimes we try to hide things we've done. Like trying to hide ice cubes from view, it's painful to cover up our failures and sins. And like trying to hide ice cubes, eventually we're found out. Maybe we can fool other people and even ourselves, but we can't fool God.** Ask a student to read Psalm 139:1-4 aloud.

Say: **God knows you—even the things you wish he didn't know. And he still loves you!** Close by praying together.

Truth *and* Consequences!

Sit in a circle. Ask a volunteer to share one time he or she lied or someone lied to him or her and what happened as a result.

Read aloud Proverbs 12:22 and 19:9. Ask:

● **What do you think the passage means by "he who pours out lies will perish"?**

Say: **Lies always have negative results—even if it takes a while. More importantly, God hates lies, but he is happy with those who are honest.**

Make a pop-up puppet. Fold a 6x6-inch piece of paper in half. In the center of the fold, make a one-inch horizontal cut. Fold the two flaps back to form triangles. Keep folding the triangles back and forth like a hinge. Open the paper, and pop the two triangles inward. These will form the lips. Draw a face around the lips, and add eyes and a nose. Next, make two vertical slits on opposite sides of the face for your thumb and pointer finger to work the puppet mouth. Help kids make their own puppets.

Have the kids sit in groups of three with their puppets. Have kids take turns using the puppets to make false statements. After a statement is made, the other two trio members brainstorm as many consequences for the lie as possible. One example might be:

Statement: "No, Dad—I didn't break that window."

Consequences: Dad loses trust in you; you may lose privileges for your lie; God is disappointed in you; someone else gets blamed; Dad finds out later and you get in double trouble for breaking the window and for lying.

After the other trio members have finished brainstorming, have the puppet tell the truth and have the other trio members list the consequences of being honest. Give each member of the trio a chance to use his or her puppet.

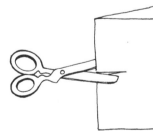  

Chapter Five

Kindness

Kindness is a gift that is given and received back at the same time. It involves taking part of our personal resources and investing in another person's comfort, happiness, or welfare. Whether it is a smile or half of our last candy bar, we choose to give something up with the simple intent of making someone else happy. When the value of our contribution is affirmed by that person's response, it feels great!

When kids first discover kindness, it gives them a sense of real power: they realize that something they do can have an impact on another person. As people respond favorably to their efforts, their desire to be kind grows. Unfortunately, as acts of kindness are overlooked or unappreciated, the desire to be kind diminishes. But the good news is this: God appreciates kindness, even when others don't. He works through human kindness, too. When we encourage and reward kindness, we give kids what they need to bloom.

These activities give kids a chance to practice kindness and understand biblical reasons that they should. Be abundant in your praise and encouragement, especially as you notice kindness becoming spontaneous in your kids' lives.

● ● ●

The Extra Mile

Gather kids in a circle. Call out a common chore, such as washing dishes. Have the kids who do this chore regularly at home step to the center and pantomime the chore as those who are left in the circle count to five. Then re-form the circle. Repeat this with five to ten other chores. Then ask:

- **Do you like to do chores? Why or why not?**
- **What do you do when you finish your chores?**
- **Do your parents ever ask you to do extra chores? Explain.**

Say: **The Bible tells of a young woman named Rebekah who got water for her family by filling her jar with water from a spring. One time when Rebekah came to the spring, one of Abraham's servants was resting by the water. The servant asked Rebekah to give him a sip of water from her jar.**

Have kids get into groups of four. Ask a volunteer in each group to read Genesis 24:18-20 aloud to his or her group to see how Rebekah responded to the servant's request. Have groups discuss these questions:

- **What did Rebekah do beyond her normal chore of filling her water jar?**
- **Why do you think Rebekah did these things?**
- **How do you think that made Abraham's servant feel?**
- **What are some extra things you can do to help out at your home?**
- **How will doing those things make your family feel?**

Say: **Chores are the things we do because we need to contribute to our family. Service in our families doesn't begin until we go beyond our regular responsibilities.**

Pass out index cards, and have the kids each trim about one-fourth of an inch off the long side of the cards. Then have them each write or draw pictures of several things they could do to serve their families on the rest of the index card. Provide glitter glue or ribbon to glue around the edges as a border. Have kids each make a case for their service projects by cutting one index card in half widthwise

and stapling it to the bottom half of a full index card, being careful to staple at the very edges. Suggest that they keep these in a safe place so that they can use the ideas as they have an opportunity.

A Drop of Kindness

Have kids get in groups of three to discuss these questions:
● **What's the nicest thing anyone has ever done for you?**
● **How did that person's act make you feel?**
● **What's the nicest thing you've ever done for someone else?**
Give each child a clear-plastic cup filled with water, and set out bottles of food coloring. Have each child put one drop of food coloring in his or her cup. Ask kids to watch the drops as they work their way through the water. Then have kids each add more drops of the same color in their glasses. Have trios discuss these questions:
● **How did your drop of food coloring change the water?**
● **How many drops of food coloring did it take to change the water?**
● **How many acts of kindness does it take to change the way someone feels?**
● **How is the change in the water like what our acts of kindness do for other people? How is it different?**
Have a volunteer read Mark 9:41 aloud. Ask:
● **How big or expensive does an act of kindness need to be in order to be important to God?**
● **Why would God give us a reward just for giving someone else a cup of water?**
Pour each child a fresh cup of water as you remind children that even small acts of kindness are important to God. Before they drink, have each child tell a partner a small thing they could do to show kindness before they go to bed tonight.

Clothed With Kindness

Do this activity in conjunction with a clothing drive your church has planned, or plan ahead to have kids collect clothes to give to a local shelter program. This activity serves to sort the clothes as well as teach an important lesson.
Place all the donated items in one area of the room. Provide large pieces of newsprint and markers, and have the children work in pairs

to trace each other's whole bodies on the paper.

Read Colossians 3:12 aloud.

Ask:

● **What do you think it means to "clothe yourself with... kindness"?**

Say: **Now let's cover our pictures according to the verse we just read. Choose items from the clothing we have collected, and clothe your traced body.** Go through each word mentioned in the verse, and have kids select an item of clothing that reminds them of that word. For example, for compassion, one child may choose a soft sweater and another may choose a pair of socks. Have them each tell their partners why they chose that particular item before you call out the next word.

Say: **You got a chance to act out that Bible verse in a way that will help you to remember it, but really, this whole activity is based on an act of kindness. Those who donated clothing to be given away have acted in kindness, and as we gather this clothing back together, we are doing a kindness for those who will have to sort it for distribution.** Have the kids bring up clothing a single item at a time, and bag all similar items together. Then have kids create labels to indicate what is inside each bag as an act of kindness and consideration for the recipients. (Hint: Be careful not to separate outfits.)

Kindness Baskets

Before class, gather strawberry baskets, ribbon, small boxes of crayons, balloons, and trinkets that will fit inside the baskets. You may also want tissue paper or artificial grass to pad each basket.

Read Ephesians 4:32a aloud. Then ask:

● **What does the word compassionate mean?**

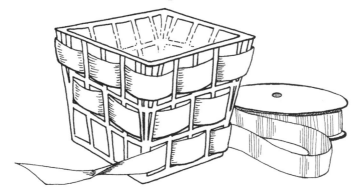

● How does it fit in with kindness?

● When might people especially need to be shown kindness and compassion?

Say: **Today we're going to make Kindness Baskets to keep at church for times when we need to show kindness and compassion to other children. It might be when they are visiting, or sick, or at a time they feel especially sad.** Set out the strawberry baskets, ribbon, scissors, and glue. Show the children how to weave ribbon through the holes in the baskets. When they are finished, fill the baskets with the gift items you have collected. Store the finished baskets where they can be used as needed.

Service Suggestions Box

Before class, find a shoe box or a facial tissue box. Cut out five pieces of poster board to correspond with the box's sides and top (make an opening in the top section).

Have children form five groups, and give each group one poster-board piece, some markers, and some stickers. Ask a volunteer in each group to read aloud Matthew 25:34-40. Then ask:

● **What is this passage asking us to do?**

● **How can we be kind to others?**

Ask groups to decorate their poster-board pieces to reflect the passage's message. Then glue the pieces to the box to create a Service Suggestions Box. As the glue dries, ask:

● **What are some things people in our church may need help with? People in your school? People in your neighborhood?**

● **How can we work together to help others?**

● **What can you do by yourself to help others?**

Give each group several strips of paper to write down service ideas. Have the groups put their ideas into the Service Suggestions Box. Then discuss how you'd like to incorporate the service suggestions into your regular meetings. For example, you could have a volunteer choose a slip from the box once a month, or you could read through the suggestions once a week and discuss simple ways to make service to others a daily part of children's lives. Encourage children to add to the Service Suggestions Box on a regular basis.

101 Ways to Be Kind

Gather children around you, and ask:
● **Have you ever been to a place where you didn't know anyone?**
● **How does it feel to be a stranger?**
Say: **A woman in the Bible named Ruth was a stranger in a land far away from her home. She didn't know anyone, and she even looked different from everyone else.**
Ask for a few volunteers to read Ruth 2:4-16 aloud. Ask:
● **How was Boaz kind to Ruth?**
● **How do you think Ruth felt when Boaz invited her to stay in his fields? When he offered her water and food?**
Have children get into groups of four, and give each group a stack of index cards and markers. Challenge children to think of as many acts of kindness as they can—anything from a smile to mowing a neighbor's lawn—and write or draw each act on an index card. Then have groups tell about their ideas. Collect the cards, and ask each child to commit to performing one act of kindness during the week.

Before the next class, photocopy the index cards and create a 101 Ways to Be Kind booklet for each child. Use the reproducible cover included here (p. 51), or create your own. Bind the cards with a ring or twisted chenille wire. Challenge kids to add to their booklets and to regularly perform the acts of kindness listed in them.

101 Ways to Be Kind

Growing Kindness

Before class, collect a small flowerpot for each child. You may want to ask church members for unused pots, purchase pots from a garden or discount store, or ask a store for donations of cracked flowerpots. You'll also need to collect potting soil; small plants; permanent or paint markers; water; clear, matte acrylic varnish; and paintbrushes. Cover a table with newspaper, and set up the supplies.

Have children each select a flowerpot and write their names on newspaper next to their pots. Then have children go from pot to pot, using the markers to write or draw something they appreciate about each person on that person's flowerpot. After they have each added a kindness to each pot, have a volunteer read aloud Romans 12:10. Ask:

● **What does it mean to honor one another?**
● **How do you feel when someone is kind to you?**
● **Why do you think God wants us to be kind to one another?**

Help kids use the acrylic varnish to seal their pots and then place small plants and some potting soil into their pots. Say: **Think of ways that you can honor someone outside our class this week.** Ask:

● **What can you do to honor him or her?**

Say: **Just as the markers will leave a lasting mark on the flowerpots, the messages will leave a lasting mark on each one of you. Good things happen when we honor each other and are kind to each other.**

Lydia's Purple Party

Invite a group of any age, from younger kids to elderly members, for a get-together with your kids. Set a date, and send out invitations on purple paper.

Since Lydia was a merchant of purple cloth, that will be your theme! You'll need purple paper (or white paper that kids color purple), purple crayons, scissors for each child, tape, and adding machine tape or crepe paper that can be used to make streamers.

If your time is limited, you may want to make the decorations during one meeting and then actually hold the party at another time.

Serve Lydia's Liquid (grape soda poured over vanilla ice cream), white cake with purple frosting, thumb-print cookies with grape-jelly centers, or other purple treats.

Gather the kids together. Say: **When the Christian church was brand-new, Paul traveled from country to country telling people about Jesus and organizing churches. When he went to a place called Macedonia, in Europe, he met a woman named Lydia. Lydia was a merchant who sold beautiful purple cloth.**

Have one (or several) kids read Acts 16:13-15 aloud. Then ask:

● **Why do you think Lydia invited Paul and his companions into her home?**

● **How do you think this made Paul and his companions feel?**

● **How did Lydia's hospitality help the early church?**

Say: **One of the ways that we, as Christians today, can show kindness is through our hospitality. We are going to celebrate Christian hospitality by hosting Lydia's Purple Party.**

Demonstrate how to make Lydia's Lace by folding a piece of purple paper into thirds or quarters and cutting away pieces, paper-snowflake fashion. When these are made, have kids use the adding machine tape or the crepe paper and purple crayons to create streamers with phrases such as "Welcome" or "Hooray for Lydia!" As the kids work, explain who will be coming to the party. Ask kids to tell you ways that they can show hospitality to the guests. Discuss manners and serving as ways to demonstrate kindness. When the decorations are finished, have some of the kids tape them around the room while others help you set out the refreshments.

When the guests arrive, have your kids explain who Lydia was and why the room is decorated in purple.

Before the refreshments are served, ask everyone to join hands. Pray: **Dear God, Lydia invited Paul and his companions into her home. She showed Christian hospitality when the church was brand-new. We had fun decorating this room with purple decorations in her honor. We're glad to be hosts to our guests today, and we thank you for this food. Amen.**

Encourage your guests, especially if they are older, to tell of a time they have had kindness expressed to them through hospitality.

Baby Moses in a Basket

Your kids will each make a Baby Moses Basket to give to a younger child at church. Decide when your group will meet with the younger kids to do a Buddy Share, either right after they finish making the baskets or at another time.

For each child you'll need: a paper plate, a brown crayon, a twelve-inch piece of ribbon, a picture of a baby's face (from a magazine or a photo) and a 5x5-inch square cut from an old receiving blanket. You'll also need a stapler, a hole punch, and glue.

Begin by asking:

● **Tell me about a time you helped a baby or a younger child.**

● **Was it easy or was it difficult?**

● **How did you feel helping the child?**

Say: **Today we're going to learn about a young woman in the Bible who showed great kindness to a baby. The king of Egypt didn't like the Hebrews and declared that all the baby boys were to be killed. This is the story of how one of those babies was saved.**

Have someone read aloud Exodus 2:1-10. Then ask:

● **Why do you think the king's daughter tried to help the baby?**

Say: **We can show kindness by caring for those who are younger**

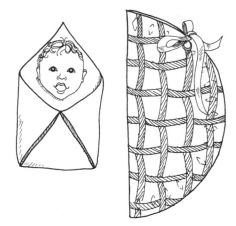

than we are. Today you are going to make something to give to a younger child at our church. (Explain which group kids will be doing the Buddy Share with and when they'll be sharing.)

Tell the kids to color both sides of the paper plates to look like baskets. Have them each fold a paper plate in half and staple one side of the paper plate together around the edges. Tell kids each to leave the other side of their paper plates open and have them each punch a hole through both halves of the open side to tie with a ribbon. Have kids each hold their blanket squares so that one of the points is aimed at their tummies. Then have kids each glue a picture of a baby's face about an inch below the top corner of the blanket. Show kids how to fold the bottom corner of the blanket up toward the baby's face and then fold in each of the side corners as though they are swaddling real babies. Then they can place the babies inside the baskets and tie the baskets closed.

Before the younger kids arrive, have your kids hide the Baby Moses Baskets around the room, in a larger space, or outdoors. When the younger kids arrive, pair each of your kids with a younger child for the Buddy Share. Say: **We are now on the banks of the Nile River. I believe I hear a baby crying. Buddies, check it out!**

Your kids will help their buddies look for their baskets. When a basket is found, the older Buddy in each pair will encourage the younger Buddy to open the basket and see what's inside. Then the older Buddy will tell the story of Baby Moses. After the younger Buddies leave, ask:

- **How was this activity showing kindness?**
- **How did you feel about being kind?**
- **Why would you want to be kind in the future?**

Tick-Tack-Toe With a Twist

Create a large, closed tick-tack-toe grid on the floor using masking tape. You will need six small beanbags, three marked with X's and three marked with O's.

Two children play the game at a time. One child has the X beanbags, and the other has the O's. The kids alternate tossing beanbags, trying to get three in a row. If a bag does not land on the grid, the child gets another chance. If the bag lands in a square occupied by another bag, have the child toss the beanbag again. Three in a row wins; if all the bags are tossed and three in a row is not achieved, the game is over. When other children want to play, they must ask one of the current players if they can take his or her turn during the game.

The Twist: Before the game, give several kids individual instructions. Write these out or whisper them to the children as they arrive. Instruct some kids not to let others play when they ask for a turn. Instruct others to let kids play whenever they ask for a turn. The ones who refuse a turn should continue to play the game until the teacher steps in to give others a turn.

After the game has been played several times, gather the kids together and ask how they felt if they were refused a turn. Talk with them about what it means to be kind to others. Read aloud 2 Timothy 2:24a. Ask:

- **Why do you think a servant of God should be kind?**
- **What was the kind thing to do in this game?**
- **What are some ways you can be kind?**

Cheery Kindness Card!

As the kids come in, have them sit on the floor in a circle. Ask:
- **What are some of the kindest things people have done for you?**
- **When do you need a little kindness?**

Read Proverbs 12:25 aloud. Ask:
- **What do you think an "anxious heart" might be?**

Say: **Think of someone you know who might have an anxious heart right now. We are going to make some cards that could be words of cheer to those people.**

Give kids each a piece of construction paper, and have them fold the paper in half. On the outside of the card, have kids each draw a colorful picture. On the inside, have them copy this little poem:

> We all need a little kindness
> To help us on our way;
> So here's a special treat
> To make you smile today!

The kids can then sign the cards "Someone who thinks you're terrific!" or "A friend." Attach a wrapped granola bar or some other small treat to the inside-front cover of each card.

Encourage the kids to give these to people without revealing who did it.

Chapter Six

Love

Love is such a small word to carry the immense meaning we pour into it! We use the word love to mean everything from "having a distinct preference for..." (as in "I love chocolate") to a one-word summary for the nature of the living God.

Love as a Christian character-trait involves a demonstration of God's character expressed in ways humans can grasp. Our acts of love become a tangible connection to the heart of God for those around us. His Word leaves no doubt that love is both our privilege and our responsibility as his children.

Activities in this chapter will help kids see God's love and express it through their actions. Throughout this chapter, it's important to remind kids that love is a choice and that the *feeling* of love is a benefit that comes along with its expression.

● ● ●

Love Comes A-Cross

Prepare a construction paper cross for each child. Make each arm of the cross two inches wide with the crosspieces and the top two inches long and the bottom four and one half inches long. The finished cross should be eight and one half inches tall and six inches wide.

Ask:

● **What is love?**

Then say: **Here's something the Bible says about love.** Read aloud 1 John 3:16-18. Ask:

● **What does that tell us about love?**

● How can we love others with our actions?

Say: **One way to show love to others is through giving.**

Have children write the words on the crosses as shown in the illustration. Then have them fold the crosses into boxes, with the words inside. On the top of each box, have kids write: "Open and unfold box to receive a message of love."

Have kids decorate the outside of their boxes as much as they want to and then place a candy treat or two inside the box. Say: **God showed us his love by giving his only Son to die on the cross. We follow his example in a tiny way when we give to others.**

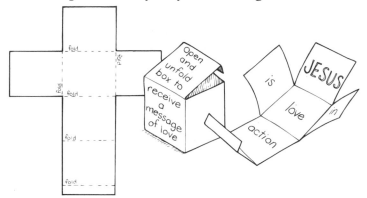

Awesome Love

This activity works best with kids who can read fairly well. Form groups of about four. Make sure you have at least one good reader in each group. Have them read Romans 5:6-8. Then say: **Now you're all going to become sign language creators. In your group, create some sign language symbols to show the thoughts of this Bible passage.**

Give groups five to ten minutes to prepare their presentations and then have each group sign its message to the rest of the class. Ask:

● **How did it feel to sign the message of this passage?**

● **What do these presentations and the Bible passage tell us about God's love?**

● **What did Jesus do for us by dying on the cross?**

● **How does God want us to respond to his love?**

Say: **God loves us so much that he sent his only Son to die on the cross so that we could go to heaven. And God wants us to trust in Jesus so that we can live with him forever.**

If you have children who have never expressed faith in Jesus, now might be a good time to explain to them how they can do that.

Love Bubbles

Gather heart-shaped cookie cutters, floral wire cut into pieces long enough to go around the outside edge of a cookie cutter plus three inches for the tail, scissors, thick chenille wires, and bubble liquid.

Have the kids make bubble blowers. Give each child a length of the floral wire, a cookie cutter, and a thick chenille wire. Have kids shape the wire around the outsides of the cookie cutters, leaving two "tails" of equal length. Tell kids to twist the tail ends together and remove the floral wire from the cookie cutters. Have kids twist the tails around the chenille wires. Bring out the bubble liquid in a bowl, and have the kids blow heart-shaped bubbles to show each other their love.

Read 1 John 4:19-21 aloud. Say: **Because God loves us, he thinks it's important that we love each other.** Ask:
- **Why can we love others?**
- **If we love God, what will we do?**
- **Who is someone you can show love to when you leave here? How?**

Say: **Sometimes it's fun to show others love. Sometimes it's hard. God wants us to show love to others no matter what.**

Walk the Talk

Give half of the kids each an index card with an emotion written on it. (Some examples are "happy," "sad," "angry," and "worried.") Line the kids who have cards up on one side of the room. Explain that when you say "go," each child should act out the emotion on his or her card in any way he or she can without saying the word.

Give each of the remaining kids a pencil and a piece of paper. Explain that when you say "go," it is their job to guess what emotion each person in the first group is acting out. As they watch the actors, they should each write down the person's name and a guess about what emotion he or she is demonstrating. Have them keep their guesses to themselves and sit down when they are finished.

When kids in the second group are finished guessing, name each actor and your guess about the emotion he or she was acting out. Make sure your guess is obviously wrong. For example, you may announce that Sheri (who was acting happy) was representing anger or that John (who was acting sad) was representing happiness. As the kids respond with surprise or disbelief, ask:

● **Why don't you believe my answers are correct?**
Ask the first group:
● **How did you try to get the second group to guess your emotion?**
Ask the second group:
● **How did you decide what emotion to guess?**

Read aloud John 13:35. Say: **Even though I said (child's name) was angry and (child's name) was happy, you didn't believe me because that's not the way they acted. This verse helps us understand that our words and actions have to match. If we say we are followers of Jesus but we don't show love in our actions, no one will believe us. But if we act with love toward others, people will know we follow Jesus even if we don't tell them.**

Love Links!

Have kids sit in a row. Say: **I have some great news for you today! The Bible says that no matter what is going on in our lives—good things or bad things—God will always love us and nothing can separate us from his love.**

Read Romans 8:35-39 aloud.

Say: **God's love will never fail us! We are "chained" to God and to the love of Christ for eternity. The Bible says that nothing can separate us from God's love. Ask:**

- How does that make you feel?
- What are some things that could cause people to *feel* separated from God?

Brainstorm a list with the kids. Reread Romans 8:35-39 for some good ideas. Examples might include trouble, hardship, people being mean, famine, being poor, danger, or weapons. Ask:

- Even though these things can cause us to take our eyes off God, what does the Bible say about his love?

To help kids remember this passage, play the following game. Have the first person jump up and name one thing from the list or a new idea and say, "(Bad thing) won't separate me from the love of God!" Have that person clasp his or her hands together and put his or her arms straight out to form a "link." Continue with another person doing the same thing, only this time he or she will put the link formed over the head and shoulders of the first person. Keep going until everyone is joined. The last person will link to the first person, forming a circle. As you stand together, thank God for joining you in his great love.

Love List

Have the kids sit facing the chalkboard or chart paper. Read aloud Matthew 5:43-48. Ask:

- What does Jesus say about our enemies?
- How is this different from the way we normally think of our enemies?
- Why is this so hard to do?

On the chalkboard or chart paper, make a Love List. At the tops of two separate columns, write "Who is my enemy?" and "How can I love my enemy?" Encourage the kids to name enemies by action, not by name. Kids might list people such as "someone who calls me names," "someone who cheats off my paper," or "someone who hits me." Then, next to each enemy, list how you can show love. Kids might say things such as "compliment them," "offer to help them study for the next test," "tell an adult," or "pray for them."

After the list has been brainstormed, have the kids take turns role playing these situations in pairs. Once they've gotten the hang of it, throw in some new situations.

Say: **Jesus has challenged us to be patient with our enemies and to** be peacemakers. Remember, we're to be good examples of Jesus' attitude for other people to see. If you love your enemies, you'll certainly be a great example of the way we love because God loved us first.

Loving Our Neighbors

Assist children in making a batch of Gift Cookies, using the following recipe. Be sure to multiply the recipe as needed. Each batch is about equal to one package of refrigerated sugar-cookie dough, if you prefer to use it.

Gift Cookies
1/2 cup butter
1 cup sugar
1 egg
1 tablespoon milk
1/2 teaspoon vanilla
1 1/2 cups flour
1 teaspoon baking powder
1/4 teaspoon salt

Mix all the ingredients. Roll the dough into a large rectangle. Cut the rectangle into three large, flat, rectangular-shaped cookies. Bake at 350 degrees for 12 to 15 minutes. This makes enough dough for two or three gift cookies.

While the cookies are baking, read Matthew 22:39 aloud and then ask:
● **What's a neighbor?**
● **Who are your neighbors?**
● **Who are our neighbors in this church?**
● **What are some things we can do to love our neighbors?**
Say: **One way we can show love to our neighbors is by giving them gifts. Let's make some gifts for our neighbors in this church.**

When the cookies are done baking and have cooled somewhat, set out frosting, small candies, sprinkles, and other supplies, and instruct each child to decorate a cookie to look like a gift.

Have children place their cookies on decorative paper plates that say, "Love your neighbor as yourself" on them. Then lead kids in serving their cookies to another class.

Loving Our Enemies

Instruct kids to each choose a color of construction paper that represents a person he or she loves. Help each child tear a heart shape out of the paper. Have kids form a circle and take turns telling who their heart shapes represent.

Read Matthew 5:44 aloud and then ask:
- **What is an enemy?**
- **Why do you think Jesus wants us to love our enemies?**
- **What are some ways we can love our enemies?**

Hang a large piece of plain, wrinkled, or faded paper on the wall. Tell kids that this paper represents people who aren't so easy to love — people who might be considered enemies. Say: **Let's make a collage to see what it might be like to show our enemies the same kind of love we show to the things or people we like best.**

Provide additional art supplies, and instruct children to work together to make a collage by pasting their paper hearts over the paper on the wall and adding other decorations. Ask:
- **What has happened to the paper?**
- **How is this like what happens when we are loving to our enemies?**

Say: **Even this ugly paper was made more beautiful by our symbols of love. Imagine how great the change can be when we are loving to other people!**

Bouquet of Love

Gather the children around a vase of flowers. Talk about the tradition of giving a bouquet of flowers to express love. Read 1 John 3:18 aloud. Then ask:
- **What are some actions people do for you that make you feel loved?**
- **What are some actions you could do to show your love for others?**

Say: **God desires for our love to be active, so let's make a bouquet to help remind us to show our love.** Give each child three craft sticks. Have them write on each stick something they could do for another that would express love. Some ideas might include: doing a chore for a sibling, doing a job around the house without being asked,

or sharing something very precious with a friend. Have kids cut out four small hearts per stick. Then have kids glue the four hearts into a flower shape at the end of each stick. Tell kids to glue or tape a wrapped candy to the center of each flower. Pass out cups and modeling dough for each person. Have kids push the dough into the cups and then stick the stick flowers into the dough.

Children may want to label the flowers for specific people to match the loving actions. They also may want to make extra flowers if they have more than three people in mind.

Encourage the kids to pull the flowers from their cups during the coming week. As they complete loving acts, they can reward themselves with the candy flower-centers.

Banner of Love

Say: **God's Word is full of verses that express his love for us. When life gets difficult, we can remember God's wonderful love and feel encouraged.** Have several children read the following verses about God's love toward us: Psalm 86:15; Song of Songs 2:4; Isaiah 54:10; Jeremiah 31:3; Romans 5:8; Romans 8:38-39; Ephesians 2:4-5; and 1 John 3:1a. Then ask:
- **How does God feel about you?**
- **How does this make you feel?**

Help children each create a banner to hang in a place where it will remind them to remember God's love for them.

Give each child a piece of craft foam (available in sheets at most craft-supply stores) and a dowel. The dowels should be two inches

He has taken me to
the banquet hall,
and
his banner over
me is love.

Song
of Songs
2:4

longer than the width of the foam. Have kids each fold the edge of the foam where the dowel will go through and cut vertical slits every one to two inches. The slits need to be only as long as the width of the dowel. Tell kids to thread the dowel through the slits and cut fringe along the bottom edge of the foam. Let the children cut out foam shapes and designs to glue onto their banners. Have them each use permanent markers to write one of the verses on the banner. Encourage kids to write all the verse references on the backs of their banners. Have them each tie a ribbon to the two ends of the dowel to use as a hanger. Let kids embellish their banners with curling ribbons hanging from the sides, glue-on sequins, or other craft items.

Chapter Seven

Respect

Respect forms the platform for obedience, courtesy, and order in our relationships and our society. It is often said that respect must be earned, but God's principles go beyond that. We treat others with respect as an extension of our respect for God. Because he is the Creator, we respect his creation and his plans to govern our lives.

The activities in this chapter will help kids identify actions that show respect. When kids are clear about the importance of respect, they'll be able to develop healthy boundaries for their behavior. They'll also be able to filter the behavior of others as they learn self-respect that comes from valuing themselves as God sees them.

● ● ●

Protected Property

Give kids each a chunk of modeling clay. Have them each create something that symbolizes something about themselves. For example, someone who likes basketball might create a miniature basketball. Someone who gets good grades might make a letter A.

Give kids a few minutes to create and then have kids explain what they made and line up their creations on a table at the front of the room. Say: **You really put a lot of work into these creations, but I could carelessly toss a book down on top of them or spill a drink on them. Anyone could ruin them quickly and easily just by being careless, or, worse yet, they could ruin them on purpose. Your creations are sitting out here unprotected, and they are in serious danger.** Ask:

● **How easy would it be for me or someone else to damage your creations?**

● Why do you think I would or wouldn't actually harm them?

Say: **Let's look at a story that tells about someone important who was in a situation similar to that of your creations.** Read aloud 1 Samuel 24:1-10. Ask:

● **Saul was out to kill David; why do you think David didn't kill Saul when he had the chance?**

● **Why did David even feel bad about cutting off a piece of Saul's robe?**

● **How does our respect for others show itself in the way we treat each other?**

● **How can we show more respect for each other? For our teachers? For our parents?**

Say: **We are God's creations. God feels the same kind of protectiveness toward us that we feel toward something we work hard on. God gave us a great example of the kind of respect he'd like to see us show in this story about David and Saul.**

Accepted Authority

When kids have all arrived, begin by giving them the following orders (or similar ones that fit your situation better). Say: **Everyone stand facing the back wall. Sit down in your chairs. Stand and form one big circle. Sit down on the floor right where you are. Trade places with the person across the circle from you. Return to your seat.**

After each order, pause until kids comply. After the last order, ask:

● **How did you feel being ordered around like that?**

● **Why did you do what I said?**

Read aloud Matthew 8:5-13. Ask:

● **How is what we just did similar to what the centurion described in this story?**

● **Why did the centurion respect Jesus' authority?**

● **Why should we respect Jesus' authority?**

● **What does it mean to respect Jesus' authority?**

● **How can we be more respectful of Jesus?**

Say: **Jesus has the power to do anything. He spoke and our world was created. We respect his authority by obeying what he asks us to do and by turning to him when we have needs.**

One Wise Woman

Lead kids in doing the motions to this interactive Bible story. If you have older children, let them take turns reading portions of the story aloud and leading others in the motions. You can even have children take the roles of Nabal, David, David's men, and Abigail and act out the story as you read it aloud.

Nabal was a wealthy man who lived up to his name. (*Puff out your chest proudly and grasp imaginary lapels.*)

His name meant "fool," and that he was (*twirl your index finger near your ear to indicate "crazy"*);

And meanness was his game! (*Hold up your fists.*)

David was a mighty man who soon would be the king. (*Place an imaginary crown on your head.*)

He loved the Lord with all his heart (*fold your hands and look up*)— **More than anything!** (*Spread your arms wide.*)

One day Nabal got a call from ten of David's men. (*Hold up ten fingers.*)

"We've watched your shepherds faithfully (*hold your hand over your brow, as if searching*);

No harm has come to them. (*Shake your head "no."*)

Night and day we watched them," the men said honestly. (*Pretend to sleep on your hands and then stretch.*)

"We didn't steal a single thing (*pretend to sneak something into a pocket*);

Just ask them, and you'll see! (*Shake your index finger.*)

Since David's army helped you out—and did it all for free (*point to another person*)—

We wondered if you'd share your food. (*Pretend to eat.*)

Our men are so hungry!" (*Rub your tummy.*)

But Nabal scoffed and shook his head as if he didn't care. (*Push your hands away and shake your head.*)

"Why should I give my bread and meat (*put your hands on your hips*)

To men from who-knows-where?" (*Hold your hands up and shrug.*)

When David heard what Nabal did, he said, "This isn't right!" (*Hold your hand to your ear.*)

He told his men, "Put on your swords! (*Pretend to strap on a sword belt.*)

This Nabal we will fight!" *(Draw an imaginary sword and hold it high.)*

Now Abigail was Nabal's wife—and she was very wise. *(Touch your finger to your temple.)*

When she heard what her husband did *(hold your hand to your ear),*

She knew she had to fly! *(Point to an imaginary watch.)*

She loaded up her donkeys with two hundred loaves of bread *(pretend to carry a heavy load),*

Some wine, some sheep, and some roasted grain *(pretend the load gets heavier with each item),*

Then sent them on ahead. *(Point in front of you.)*

She rode behind the donkeys 'til she spotted David's men. *(Pretend to ride a "bouncy" donkey.)*

Abigail was brave and wise *(flex your muscles and then point to your temple)*

Do you know what she did then? *(Point to someone.)*

She quickly left her donkey and knelt at David's feet *(kneel);*

She bowed her head down very low *(bow your head);*

And said, "My lord, blame me. *(Put your hand on your chest.)*

Ignore my wicked husband—that fool was very rude! *(Point behind you, indicating Nabal is back home.)*

If I had seen the men you sent *(point to yourself),*

I would have shared our food. *(Hold out your hands.)*

I know you are a mighty man—a man who loves the Lord. *(Flex your muscles and then fold your hands in prayer.)*

Please forgive your servant *(point to yourself),*

And put away your sword." *(Put away an imaginary sword.)*

Wise Abigail had shown respect and saved her household, too. *(Point to your temple.)*

Respect is something everyone *(hold out your arms to indicate everyone in the room)*

Can show today. Can you? *(Point to someone.)*

When you finish reading the story, ask:

● **Why should Nabal have treated David with respect?**

● **How did Abigail show respect to David?**

Have a volunteer read aloud 1 Peter 2:17 from an easy-to-understand Bible translation. Then ask:

● **Who does this verse say that we should respect?**

● **Who is someone you can show respect to today? How?**

Say: **God made people and God wants us to respect his creation.**

This week, remember that Nabal—the fool—wasn't respectful. Let's follow Abigail's example—she was one wise woman!

Valuable Treasure

Before this activity, collect about ten dollars in change. You'll want a healthy pile of pennies, nickels, dimes, and quarters. Place your money in some kind of a treasure box, locked bank, shiny box, or other fancy container.

Form a circle, and have kids sit down. Hold up your treasure container, and say: **I've brought in a real treasure today. What do you think might be in here?** Allow a minute for kids to guess and then pour the change into a pile in the middle of the circle. Ask:

● **What are some things we can do with this money?**

● **Why is this money a treasure?**

Say: **This reminds me of another treasure we all have—God's Word.** Hold up a Bible. **Let's look at Psalm 119 to learn about the treasure of God's Word.**

Have a few volunteers read aloud the following Scripture passages:

● Psalm 119:33

● Psalm 119:62

● Psalm 119:97-98

● Psalm 119:105

● Psalm 119:164-165

Point to the pile of money, and say: **You told me lots of reasons that this money is a treasure.** Hold up a Bible, and ask:

● **Why is God's Word a treasure?**

Point to the pile of money, and say: **You told me lots of things to do with that treasure.** Hold up a Bible, and ask:

● **What can we do with this treasure?**

Point to the treasure container, and ask:

● **How did I treat my pile of change?**

Hold up the Bible, and ask:

● **How should we treat this treasure?**

● **Why should we treat God's Word with respect?**

● **How can you show this respect?**

Say: **God's Word is the most valuable treasure we have. This pile of change can be spent or used up. But God's Word stays with us forever. That's why it's so important to treat it with respect—**

because it's something special.

Put the change back into its box, and place the Bible in the center of the circle. Say: **Let's pray and thank God for giving us the precious treasure of his Word.** Lead children in praying and thanking God for the Bible.

You Can't Tell a Book by Its Cover

Ask children each to cut out pictures of three people from a stack of family magazines, catalogs, or sections of newspaper. Ask your children to give you the pictures. Shuffle the pictures and then give each child two pictures.

Ask children to look at the pictures they're holding and to answer three questions:
- **Is this a nice person?**
- **Why did you answer as you did?**
- **Do you respect this person?**

Ask children to show their pictures and share their answers with the group. Point out any trends you see developing, such as "It seems people who are poorly dressed are less likely to be respected."

Then say: **I'd like you to turn on your imaginations even more. I don't have a picture of this person, but I can paint a word picture. Listen to this description, and let's answer the questions again.**

Read aloud Mark 1:4, 6. Ask:
- **Is this a nice person?**
- **Why did you answer as you did?**
- **Do you respect this person?**

Say: **You can't always tell about a person from what you see. We're quick to reach conclusions without taking time to get to know people. That's true in our friendships, and it's true in church sometimes, too. James tells us to be careful about judging people by how they look on the outside. Listen.** Ask a volunteer to read James 2:1-5 aloud. Ask:
- **Who are some people we might not respect?**
- **How can we show those people respect?**

Respect Yourself

Ask students to draw themselves on poster board or paper as they wish to appear *when they're grown up.* If they want to be scuba divers when they grow up, they can draw themselves in diving suits. If they want to be happy, ask them to draw themselves with big smiles.

When children have finished drawing, ask them to cut out the pictures with scissors so they each have a paper doll of themselves.

When children have finished cutting out their pictures, gather children in a circle. Ask them to briefly take turns showing and explaining their pictures.

Say: **I see that for all of you, you expect to be healthy when you get older. That means you need to *respect* yourself—and take care of your body. God wants you to respect your body, and there's a good reason to do so. You're made in God's own image, and if you love Jesus, your body is important!**

Ask a volunteer to read aloud 1 Corinthians 3:16-17.

Explain: **Respecting our bodies is also respecting the temple of the Holy Spirit.** Ask students to list some ways we fail to respect our bodies. As they list each item, ask children to each rip a piece off of the "body" they're holding.

When you finish listing items, ask children to hold up what's left of their dolls. Then ask:

● **What happens to our bodies when we fail to respect them?**

● **Will we be able to do what we want to do when we grow up if we don't respect our bodies? Why or why not?**

Say: **If we fail to respect our bodies, we're doing a little bit to destroy a temple of God. And it's unlikely we'll ever reach the futures we hope to have.**

Laws and Orders

Say: **When God created the world, he put "natural laws" into place. A natural law simply describes the way things work. One natural law here on earth is gravity. If I'm climbing a mountain and I step off a cliff, I'll fall. That's just how it works.**

Ask children to form trios. Ask trios to think of people—such as mountain climbers—who should especially respect gravity. Ask them to decide how they'll pantomime the people they've chosen for the rest of the group to guess. Give them one minute.

Ask trios to pantomime who they thought should respect gravity. (Parachutists will be well-represented!) Lead the class in applauding all efforts.

To check to see if gravity is still working, have everyone stand up. On the count of three, have everyone jump as high as they can.

Try this several times. While children are jumping, place a piece of plastic or a deep cake-tin on the floor in front of you. Tell children they can quit jumping because it appears that gravity is still working in your room.

Hold up an egg. Say: **Based on what you know about gravity, if I drop this egg, what will happen? Right—scrambled egg. It's a natural law.**

Drop the egg.

Point out there are "spiritual laws," too—laws describing how God has set up the spiritual world. Ask for a volunteer to read aloud 2 Timothy 3:16-17.

Sum up by saying: **God gave us his Word so we'd know how to please him and so we can be ready to do good works. God's Word is true, just like gravity is true. If we ignore God's Word by breaking his laws or not obeying what Jesus says to do, it's just like ignoring gravity: we'll get scrambled! We'll be hurt by running head-on into natural laws or the spiritual laws which God has put into place.**

Ask children to list some ways they can learn God's Word. List their suggestions on a chalkboard, a dry-erase board, or on newsprint.

Close with a prayer that each child will respect God's Word, learn it, and obey it always.

Dive Into Daniel's Dip!

Have the kids sit in a circle on the floor. Summarize Daniel's story. Say: **Daniel was a slave who was being trained to be a special helper to the king. He was told to eat the rich food and drink the wine that the king gave to him. But Daniel was Jewish, and he was supposed to follow strict rules about what God said he could and couldn't eat. The king's food was not in his diet! So, out of respect for God, he chose to keep God's law and asked to be served only vegetables and water. Let's see what happened.**

Read Daniel 1:5-16 aloud, and ask:

● Do you think it was easy for Daniel to do this? Why or why not?

● Have you ever had to "go against the crowd" out of respect for what you believe? When?

Play Dive Into Daniel's Dip. Give each child a cup with ranch dressing in it and a few cut-vegetable strips. Go around the circle, and have each child offer a suggestion of how they can show respect to God by their actions. If they get stuck, give them specific situations. Examples might include:

● All your friends are talking back to their parents...

● A kid at school is being picked on by your classmates...

● You are just about to eat your supper...

After they have each given an example, tell them to take a dive into Daniel's dip!

Say: **Being respectful in a situation may take a little extra thought, but it's worth it because it pleases God.**

The Complete Picture

Before class, collect several small objects (more than one for each child). Your collection may include objects such as leaves, sponges, spools of thread, pieces of rope, small jars, and cookie cutters—anything you can dip into ink and use as a stamp.

Allow each child to choose an object he or she wants to use to create patterns on a collage.

Lay out a large piece of paper or a sheet on the floor. Provide an ink pad for every few children. Show children how to use their objects to create unique shapes on the piece of paper or the sheet. Allow them to use their objects as many times as they want to, making a large collage of shapes.

When children have finished creating their collage, ask:

● **What was it like to create this collage together?**

● **When you look at this collage, how do you feel when you see the shapes you contributed to the picture?**

● **How is this collage like our class?**

Read Philippians 2:3 aloud. Say: **Just as we need all the shapes in this picture to make the collage complete, we need all the people in this class to make the class complete. Each of you contributed a different picture to the collage, and each person brings something different to our class.** Ask:

● What does it mean to respect people who are different from you?

● How can we show respect to each other?

Say: **The more we learn to respect each other, the more we can appreciate the contributions each person makes. I'm sure that pleases God, because he loves each one of us dearly.**

Sock-Puppet Show

Before class, collect a sock for each child in class plus a few extras for visitors.

Give each child a sock and then set kids to work creating sock puppets. Provide them with buttons, glue, scissors, pieces of felt or other fabric, and yarn. While the children are working, encourage them to use their creativity to make a variety of puppets.

When children have finished creating their sock puppets, have them form a circle. Then read Exodus 20:12 aloud. Ask:

● **How can you honor your parents?**

● **Why do you think God wants you to obey your parents?**

Spend some time working with children to create a puppet show they can perform with their sock puppets about obeying parents. When kids have finished writing their puppet show, plan a time for them to perform the show for their parents or other children.

Chapter Eight

Stewardship

Stewardship is a big word for a simple concept: whatever you have, take care of it. For kids, that starts with picking up toys and being careful not to break things. As we get older, we find that the same principles apply to every area of our lives: if you're given a hand, hold it; if you're given a dollar, invest it; if you're given a day off, don't waste it; if you're given a talent, share it.

These activities will help kids see the value of who they are and what they have, regardless of what is happening with others. They will begin to see that God and others are depending on them to act responsibly for the good of all and that they may hold a puzzle piece no one else can duplicate. Nothing contributes more to a healthy self-concept than being assured that you have something valuable to offer others.

● ● ●

Tiny Bubbles

Ask:
- **How many of you have a pet?**
- **What would happen to that pet if you didn't take care of it?**

Tell children that you are going to give them each a pet bubble. Explain that kids should take care of their bubbles by protecting them from popping.

Blow bubbles across your meeting area. Tell kids to each care for one of the bubbles by blowing underneath it. Blow more bubbles as the bubbles pop, and tell kids to take care of new bubbles when they lose their old ones.

Have kids form pairs to discuss these questions:

● Was it difficult or easy to keep your bubbles from popping? Explain.

● What kinds of things do you have to take care of at home?

● What things are more difficult to care for than others? Why?

Say: **The most important thing that God has given us to take care of is each other. Listen as I read a story that shows how important this is to God.**

Read Luke 10:30-37 aloud. Then ask:

● Why do you think God wants us to take care of others?

● What's difficult about taking care of others?

● How can we take care of others?

● What are some good consequences of taking care of others?

● What are some tough parts of caring for others?

Say: **Caring for others isn't always the easiest choice. This story shows us that God cares about all kinds of people and wants us to use our talents to take care of those he loves.**

Jackpot!

Have kids form groups of four. Give each group ten of the $100,000 bills (p. 78) and a pencil. Tell children to pretend that the church has received a large donation from a member of the church and that the rich church-member has asked the people in this group to decide what should be done with the money since he can't decide for himself!

Give groups about five minutes to decide how to spend the money. Have kids indicate how each bill will be spent by writing on the back of it or by putting the bills in separate piles.

Ask groups to explain how they made decisions about spending the money they were entrusted with. Have children follow along as you read Matthew 25:14-30 aloud. Ask:

● **Did your group decide to spend the money in a way that would please God? Explain.**

● What does God want us to do with the things he gives us?

● **What do you own right now that can be used to help others and to glorify God?**

● Why does God want us to be faithful with small responsibilities before he gives us large responsibilities?

● What things, besides money, can we use to glorify God?

Tell kids that God wants them to be faithful with the little things he's given them and that they don't have to have a lot of money to make a difference for God.

What's in *Your* Hand?

Ask:

● **What are some talents, gifts, or abilities you have?**

Read 1 Peter 4:10 aloud. Ask:

● **How could you use your gifts, talents, or abilities to serve someone else? Who would that be?**

Help children plan a talent show they can perform for a class of seniors in your church, in a nursing home, or at a hospital. Be sure each child is involved in using a specific gift, talent, or ability. Outline a plan that includes making preparations for the show, preparing scenery or props, and the actual performance. As children plan and prepare for the show, talk about how using our gifts doesn't always involve being seen. Sometimes the most important things are done "behind the scenes." Invite kids to discuss ways their talent show will minister to others.

One of a Kind

Before class, instruct each child to bring a plain T-shirt or buy enough T-shirts for everyone in class. You may want to bring some extras for visitors. Set these T-shirts out on tables or the floor, placing newspaper underneath them and cardboard or thick paper between the front and back of each shirt.

Give each child half a potato and a metal cookie-cutter. Show kids how to press their cookie cutters into the cut sides of their potatoes. Then, with the help of a few adults, cut around the outsides of the cookie cutters so that the cookie-cutter shapes stand out.

Set out several containers of various colors of fabric paint. Be sure that if several children have the same cookie-cutter pattern, they have different colors of paint to use so that each person's contribution can be easily recognized. Show children how to dip their potatoes in the fabric paint, print once on a paper towel to remove excess paint, and then print on the T-shirts. Instruct each child to stamp each T-shirt once with his or her own potato printer, so that each person's shirt includes a mark from every person present.

When children are finished printing, read 1 Corinthians 12:4-7 aloud. Then ask:

● **How do you feel about the T-shirts you've created?**
● **How are these shirts like our class?**
● **How is this like us using our gifts and personalities to serve God?**

Encourage kids to view every situation in their lives as an opportunity to leave a mark for God.

Faith in Action

This improvisational play will work best with older elementary children.

Form groups of about four. Have each group read James 2:15-17 and develop a short scene that demonstrates the actions described in the passage. They may reenact the biblical story or put the message into a modern setting. Give groups about ten minutes to develop their presentations and then have them present their plays.

Ask:

● **Is there a problem with the situations you've seen here?**
● **How does God want us to respond to people in need?**
● **How can we use what God's given us to help those less fortunate than we are?**

Now have kids rejoin their groups and develop plays that depict what would please God in the same setting as their earlier plays. After about ten minutes, have kids make their presentations.

Say: **God has given us so much, and some people have so little. God is pleased when we share what we have with others who are in need.** This would be an ideal time to introduce a mission or a service project, such as a clothing collection or a canned-goods drive.

Hurry! Hurry!

Form four groups with your children. Place them in four corners of your room, or if you're outside, place them on four "bases" arranged like a baseball diamond. Say: **When I ask you to move, I want you to go to the next base to your left.**

Today you have a lot to do. You have to get up, go to school, do your chores, finish your homework, eat, and lots more. So let's get started!

Ask children to follow your actions as you go through the following routine. Make sure your actions are large and exaggerated!

Everyone stretch...it's morning! You've got the whole day ahead of you, and...argh! Look at the time! You're late! Jump out of bed! Run to the kitchen at the next base and eat breakfast! Hurry! Pour the cereal...pour the milk...shovel it down!

Run to the bus stop at the next base...wait! You're still in your pajamas! Run back home! Pull on your clothes...comb your hair...*now* run to the bus stop at the next base! Wait! You forgot to brush your teeth!

Run home again...brush up and down twenty times...now run to the bus stop...climb onto the bus...bounce up and down on the seat all the way to the next base...now run to class! Do a worksheet...read a book...raise your hand to answer a question...go sharpen a pencil...take a test...get a drink at the water fountain.

Dash to the next base — the cafeteria! Eat a sandwich...now run to PE class. Time to touch your toes...touch your nose...touch your elbows! OK, run back to class at the last base.

Study a poem...write on the chalkboard...do a math problem (count on your fingers!)...now run to the bus stop at the next base! Hurry!

Get on the bus...hurry, or it'll leave you...bounce home to the next base...do your homework...shoot baskets in the driveway...run inside and eat your dinner...hurry! Eat that broccoli! Jump into bed, and fall asleep!

Whew! What a day! Did you do a lot of stuff? Absolutely! Did you do all the important stuff? Nope—because you didn't take time to pray!

Let kids sit down. Say: **At church we talk a lot about giving money back to God. But did you know he wants us to give back our time, too? We're stewards of God's stuff. That means we don't own anything—God owns it all. But God wants us to use and take care of what he gives us, and that includes our time. God wants us to be smart in how we use our time.**

Ask a volunteer to read Ephesians 5:15-17 aloud. Say: **Doing homework and shooting baskets may please God, but praying is even more important.**

Ask:

- **In your busy day, how much time do you spend eating?**
- **How much time do you spend watching television?**

● How much time do you spend praying?

● What would happen if you switched those times around, and you spent as much time praying as you spend eating? Watching television?

Give kids each a paper plate and have them divide it into twenty-four spaces. Have them label the spaces with what fills their day and night. Have kids each punch a hole in the center of their paper plates and then have them each cut an arrow out of construction paper and attach it with a brass fastener. Tell the kids to use the arrow to point out areas of time they could use to spend time with God each day.

Taking Care of Fluffy

Give each child an ice cube. Congratulate them on their new ice-cube pets. Ask children to name their ice cubes. Tell them the name of their new pet is "Fluffy"—unless, of course, they have a better idea!

Ask children to share the names of their pets. Ask kids who have pets at home to tell you how they take care of them.

Explain that pets need loving attention. Ask everyone to give their new pet ice-cube a big hug, then a big kiss.

Say: **Uh-oh...it looks like some of your new pets are getting smaller. Maybe there's some sort of special care we should give our new pets.** Ask:

● **What can we do to make our new pets healthier and happier?**

Affirm children's ideas, and when someone suggests placing the ice cubes in a refrigerator or freezer, quickly collect the ice cubes and remove them. Hand out paper towels to wipe up spills and for children to dry their hands on.

Say: **When someone gives us something to take care of, we must be good stewards of it. That means we take good care of it.**

Read Genesis 2:15 aloud. Say: **God put us in charge of the world. It's our job to take good care of it. Let's talk about how we can be good stewards of this giant "pet"!** Ask:

● **There are many endangered animals in the world. How can we be good stewards of them?**

● **How can we be good stewards around our own homes?**

● **How can we be good stewards in our own rooms?**

● **How can we be good stewards right here?**

Encourage children to come up with one practical idea together that they can do immediately in your classroom setting—or wherever else you are when you lead this exercise. Then do it!

Who, Me?

Before your children arrive, crumple up several dozen newspapers and scatter them around your room.

Stand outside the door of your classroom or meeting room and when your children point out that the room has been "trashed," say: **Oh, no! Look at this mess! We're supposed to have our class here, but the room is such a wreck! Help me clean it up, please.**

Hand out plastic garbage bags (you can recycle the newspaper later), and encourage children to help gather up the trash. When you've finished, ask children to gather in a circle. Sit with them. Confess that you trashed the room so you could see if they'd help clean up the mess. Then ask:

● **How did you feel when I asked you to clean up a mess you hadn't made?**

● **Have you ever cleaned up a mess at home made by a brother or a sister or a parent? How did it feel to do that?**

● **Does anyone ever ask you to clean up your room? Who? How often?**

Ask a volunteer to read Genesis 2:15 and Genesis 4:9 aloud. Say: **The answer to the second question is, "yes, you *are* your brother's keeper!"** It's your job to take care of God's creation even if others *don't* take care of it.

Ask children to list some of the ways people don't take care of what they've been given.

Say: **God wants us to take good care of what he's given us to be "good stewards." That means we sometimes have to clean up the mess left by other people, whether it's a little mess in our homes or a big mess that affects the whole world.**

Let's think of ways we can care for our world in the same way we all pitched in and cleaned up this room. Encourage children to brainstorm doable ideas. Keep a list and incorporate them throughout the coming year.

Bank on It!

Have the kids sit in a circle. Read Proverbs 13:11 aloud. Ask:

● **What is honest money?** (Kids may say things such as "money earned by doing work.")

● **What is dishonest money?** (Kids may say things such as "money you found and kept without trying to find the real owner," "money that you secretly save from your lunch money," or "money that isn't used wisely.")

● **What does God say in this passage about being a good steward of our money?**

Say: **God is pleased when we are good stewards of our money and when we give back some of the money we earn to him by giving to the church or to the needy.**

Give each child four containers. These can be soup cans, baby-food jars, potato chip canisters, or even small boxes that are the same size. Have kids cover the top of each container with a piece of cloth and then cut a small slit in the top of each fabric piece. Tell kids to hold the cloth in place with rubber bands and then bind all four of the containers together using a large rubber band. Label the four containers Spend, Invest, Give, and Goal.

As the kids work, explain that whenever they get money they should divide it into four parts. The Spend money can be used right now. The Goal money is for reaching a specific goal, like buying a toy. The Give money is at least a ten-percent tithe to be used for God's work. The Save money is to be put in a savings account or invested over many, many years. You may want to give each child ten pennies

to model how the system works.

Challenge kids to keep up this system for being honest with their money and watch what happens.

Useful Tools

Bring several useful things to class—a hammer, a tape recorder and a blank audiocassette, salt, an instant-print camera, and a spoon, for example. Set out the objects in a row on a table.

Have children get into pairs, and give each pair an index card and a pencil. Have pairs rank each item on a scale from one to ten, with "ten" being a very useful item and "one" being an item that's not useful. Encourage children to use the items; for example, children could take pictures of each other or record their voices on the audiocassette. After a few minutes, have each pair explain why it ranked the items as it did. Then ask:

● **What makes something useful?**

Ask for a volunteer to read aloud Exodus 35:30-36:1. Ask:

● **What does this passage say about how God planned to build his temple?**

● **What might have happened if Bezalel and Oholiab hadn't used their gifts to build the temple as God had instructed?**

● **How is that similar to or different from us using our tools today?**

● **How can you be a useful tool for God?**

Say: **Just as we used the items here today and just as Bezalel and Oholiab used their special gifts the way God wanted them to, you can use your special gifts for God.**

Heavenly Treasures

Hide several dollars worth of pennies around the room. Tell the children they are going on a treasure hunt and that they will be challenged to use the treasures according to God's plans. Let the children collect the pennies in pairs or trios.

Read aloud Matthew 6:19-20. Then ask:

● **What treasures do human beings collect here on earth?**

● **How long can a person enjoy these things?**

● **What can we do to store up treasures in heaven?**

Let kids pretend that the pennies are worth a dollar each. Have them count up their money. With their combined money, have kids brainstorm ideas on how to use this money wisely in storing up treasures in heaven. Have the children share their ideas with the class.

Say: **Now consider what you could do to store up treasures in heaven without having any money. God wants us to use our money wisely and generously, but what about our talents and abilities? Think of one thing you could do that could have eternal and heavenly significance.** Provide time for the children to think and share their ideas.

Give each child a penny and a piece of clear tape. Have them tape the pennies inside the front covers of their Bibles to remind them to live wisely for God's kingdom. Close by reading Matthew 6:33 aloud.

Chapter Nine

Thankfulness

An attitude of gratitude is a reward in itself. Who could offer genuine thanks without a smile? Being thankful focuses us on the positive and helps us to become happy people. It sets a tone of appreciation that brings out the best in others.

God values our thanks, too. His word is full of examples of those who have given him thanks simply because he is good! We are encouraged to balance our requests to him with thanksgiving. Thankfulness is a blessing, but it is a discipline as well. It requires that we focus outside ourselves. We have to be intentional in our search for things that are true, noble, and praiseworthy.

These activities will help kids learn the skills they need to practice intentional thanksgiving, and their lives will be richer because of it.

● ● ●

Count Your Blessings

Provide each child with a paper bag large enough to fit over his or her head, and set out plenty of art supplies such as scissors, markers, colored pencils, crayons, yarn, glue, buttons, and fabric scraps. Assign each child one of the following roles: the sun, raindrops, flowers, trees, and family members. You can assign more than one child to each role except the sun.

Show children how to use the art supplies to create paper-bag masks to fit the roles they've been assigned. Be sure children cut eyeholes in the correct places in their masks.

When children have finished making their masks, read Psalm 7:17 aloud. Then say: **We have a lot to thank God for. Let's use our masks** to participate in an interactive story about what we should be thankful to God for. When I mention your role, act out your part in the story.

Instruct children to put on their paper-bag masks. Then pray this prayer, allowing children to act out their assigned parts—wearing their masks—at the appropriate times. Say: **God has given us so many gifts. We have so many things to be thankful for. The sun comes up every morning.** Pause. **The rain falls, giving the ground the moisture it needs.** Pause. **The flowers grow and bloom.** Pause. **You, Lord, provide trees for shade.** Pause. **You give us families.** Pause. **You provide us with the things we need. You are good to us. We thank you.**

Lead children in a round of applause in thanks to God.

Kitchen-Band Worship

Before class, collect utensils from your kitchen at home or the kitchen in your church. Include utensils that will make good musical instruments, such as pots and pans, jars of beans, wooden spoons, chopsticks, bottles, glasses of water, spoons, canisters, and pan lids. Be sure you have enough instruments for each child in class plus extras for visitors.

When children arrive, read Psalm 106:1 aloud and then ask:
● **What are some ways we can express thanks to God?**
● **How do you think God feels when we praise him?**

Say: **Let's write a song and play it to praise God and thank him for his love for us.** Allow children to choose instruments to use in a worship band. Then help them write a song about thanksgiving to God. You may want to have them write new lyrics to a simple, familiar song such as "Twinkle, Twinkle, Little Star," "Old MacDonald Had a Farm," or "Jesus Loves Me."

When children have written their song, show them how to use their instruments. Then have them perform. Remind them that they are playing to God, to praise him.

You may want to have children perform their song for others in the church.

Intentional Acts of Thankfulness

You'll need aluminum foil, paper, a pen, and individually wrapped candies for this activity.

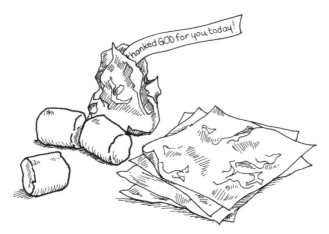

Cut out five 2x2-inch squares of aluminum foil for each child. Also make five paper flags for each child that are two inches long and one-fourth inch wide. Write "I thanked God for you today!" on each flag, or provide pens for older kids to write more personal messages of thanks.

Give each child five individually wrapped candies, five pieces of foil, and five paper flags. Have the kids wrap their candies in foil, inserting each paper flag so that it comes about halfway out of the top.

Gather in a circle, facing outward. Read aloud 1 Chronicles 16:8-9, and say: **Today we're going to give thanks to the Lord *and* give thanks to others at the same time! We're going to perform "intentional acts of thankfulness." When I tap your shoulder, place one of your candies behind someone else in the class and pray silently for that person.** Be sure every child receives a treat. As kids are giving out their candies, discuss these questions:

● **What are some of God's "wonderful acts"?**

● **What are other ways to be thankful for someone and praise God at the same time?**

After everyone receives a candy, have kids enjoy their treats. End the activity by encouraging kids to perform anonymous, intentional acts of thankfulness for people who have helped them recently. You might suggest that they put one candy secretly in the coat pocket of a brother, a sister, or a friend; place one candy on a teacher's desk; ask an adult to help them put one candy on a neighbor's doorstep; or put one candy on a parent's pillow.

If you have more class time, you might want to make larger treats by having the class bake bite-sized chocolate chip cookies. Make the paper flags bigger, and let kids write their own thank-you messages or draw "thank-you pictures."

Pulsating Praise

Use this simple model of an eardrum to help kids see their praise to God pulsate.

Have children get in groups of four. Give each group a flashlight, a stiff cardboard tube about five inches long, a piece of plastic wrap, a piece of yellow paper, a piece of paper of any other color, tape, a rubber band, and an empty cereal box.

Instruct one child in each group to tape the yellow piece of paper to the cereal box to use like a movie screen. Have the next child roll the other piece of paper like a megaphone and tape it so it stays rolled up. Give the third child a piece of plastic wrap to stretch over one end of the cardboard tube, and have him or her secure the plastic wrap with a rubber band. The wrap must be smooth across the end. The fourth child needs to tape the paper megaphone to the open end of the cardboard tube.

Have the children in each group set up the yellow-paper box facing them like a screen. Next have them lay the cardboard tube flat on the table with the plastic wrap facing the yellow paper. Have them turn on the flashlight and shine it onto the plastic wrap. The light of the flashlight should reflect off the plastic wrap onto the yellow paper. Have kids adjust the tube and the flashlight until the reflection can be seen.

Say: **What we have made here is a simple model of your eardrum. When you talk into the paper megaphone, the plastic wrap will vibrate like your eardrum vibrates. The vibrations then pass on to the three smallest bones of the body called the hammer, the anvil, and the stirrup. Those three bones vibrate and send the message to the inner ear and on to the brain. God made our sense of hearing truly amazing.**

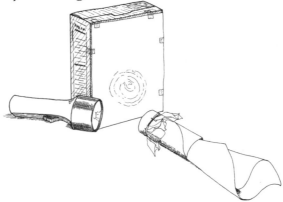

Read Psalm 139:14a aloud. Ask:
- **In what other ways has God made our bodies wonderful?**
- **How can we use our bodies to praise God?**
- **What other things are you thankful to God for?**

Have the children think of something they could say that gives praise to God. Let the children talk, shout, or sing their praise into the megaphone. Suggest trying different kinds of sounds, such as low sounds and high sounds, fast sounds and slow sounds, and so on. Watch each effect on the screen, and notice the differences.

Jumping Jamboree

Say: **Today we're going to learn about a man who rejoiced with his whole body after he was healed by the Apostle Peter in the name of Jesus. Then we will use static electricity to help our praises jump with joy.**

Read aloud Acts 3:1-10. Then ask:
- **What kind of life did this man have before he met Peter?**
- **How did he express himself after being healed?**
- **How has Jesus changed your life, and how do you express praise to God?**

Using the power of static electricity, lead the children in praising God with jumping hugs and kisses. Give each child scissors and a piece of paper to cut out X and O shapes to represent hugs and kisses The shapes should each be about the size of a one-inch square. Have kids write words on the shapes to express their praises to God. They could write down some words to describe how they feel about God, words to describe what God has done for them, words to describe things they are thankful to God for, or names of people they are thankful for.

Then give each child a large balloon to blow up and tie off. Blow the balloons up in advance for younger children. Have kids rub the balloons vigorously in their hair to create static electricity. Tell kids to place their paper praises on the table in a cluster, and have them hold their balloons over the shapes about four inches away. The shapes will jump up and down between the balloon and the table.

Encourage the children to express their thanksgiving to God with enthusiasm like the man in Acts did. Close by reading aloud 1 Thessalonians 5:18.

Thankfulness Times Ten

For this activity, you'll need a Bible, colored construction paper, scissors, and crayons or markers.

Say: **Turn to someone sitting near you, and tell about a time you thanked someone and why you thanked that person.** After a minute, call on a few children to share their responses. Then say: **There's a story in the Bible about someone who thanked Jesus. I'll need a volunteer to read the story from Luke 17:11-19.**

Have a child read the Scripture passage aloud from an easy-to-understand Bible translation. Ask:

● **How do you think Jesus felt when only one of the sick men came back to thank him?**

● **Why is it important to express our thanks?**

Say: **We're going to make thankfulness reminders to use when we pray. First, fold a sheet of paper in half. Then place your hand so that your pinkie finger lines up with the folded edge of the paper, and trace around your hand.** Demonstrate how to trace around your hand but not around the side of your pinkie. Say: **Now you'll cut around the hand shape but not on the side of your pinkie. That way, you'll make a hand-print card!** Show kids how to cut around the fingers to make cards.

When everyone has a hand-print card, say: **Now think of ten things you're thankful for, and write one of those things on each finger (or thumb!) of your card. When you pray, you can open your card and find lots of things to thank God for!**

Jerry's Birthday

Before reading the following story, tell children you'll pause often for them to participate. If they think things are going well for Jerry, they're to raise their hands, lean to the right, and shout, "Yeah!" If they think things are going poorly for Jerry, they're to lower their hands, lean to the left, and shout, "Oh no!"

The Story

It was Jerry's birthday. His parents gave him the present he wanted most: a ride in a helicopter. Pause.

Fortunately, the helicopter flew very high, so Jerry could see for miles and miles. Pause.

Unfortunately, the helicopter also bounced around in the turbulent air and Jerry fell against the helicopter door. Pause.

Unfortunately, Jerry fell out. Pause.

Fortunately, the helicopter was carrying parachutes. Pause.

Unfortunately, Jerry wasn't wearing one. Pause.

Fortunately, there was a huge lake down below Jerry. Pause.

Unfortunately, Jerry couldn't swim. Pause.

Fortunately, Jerry missed the lake. He was falling toward a farm. Pause.

Unfortunately, the farm's land was made out of dirt. *Hard dirt.* Pause.

Fortunately, on the farm there was a giant haystack. Pause.

Unfortunately, there was a pitchfork in the haystack. Pause.

Fortunately, Jerry missed the pitchfork. Pause.

Unfortunately, he also missed the haystack. Pause.

Fortunately, Jerry fell onto a flock of fluffy, chubby sheep. Pause.

Unfortunately, Jerry is allergic to wool. Pause.

Fortunately, Jerry didn't sneeze too much and he walked away from his fall. Pause.

Unfortunately, the sheep didn't. Pause.

Say: **Whew! Jerry had quite an adventure! Let's talk about it.**

● How would you have felt if *you* were Jerry?

● How do you think Jerry would have felt if he'd known everything would turn out fine *before* he fell?

Ask a volunteer to read John 14:1-3 aloud.

Say: **I'm thankful we know that no matter what happens while we're on earth, we'll spend eternity in heaven with Jesus! That means we always have something to be thankful for, even if things around us get a little crazy.**

Close with a prayer circle, asking each child to thank God for something in his or her life.

Practicing Thankfulness

Fill a bowl with small snacks such as animal crackers, grapes, M&M candies, Goldfish crackers, or raisins.

Tell children you'll practice thankfulness. Point out that the Apostle Paul was thankful for others. Paul knew that God provided for him through the kindness of others.

Ask a volunteer to read aloud 2 Corinthians 9:11.

Say: **God does a lot for us through other people in our lives, too. Let's remember some of the things others do for us as we have snacks.**

Instruct children to take just one raisin (or other snack) at a time. When a child takes a raisin, tell him or her to say, "I'm thankful for (fill in the name of a person) because (fill in a reason)." For instance, someone might say, "I'm thankful for my teacher because she tells me about Jesus."

After each child has enjoyed a few snacks, have kids form groups of no more than six. Say: **Now I'd like each of you to give another person a snack and tell that person one reason you're thankful he or she is here in our class. For instance, I'll give a raisin to Jack. I'm thankful because I enjoy Jack's sense of humor.**

One at a time in their groups, let children share snacks with each other. Be sure each child is affirmed with a round of snacks.

Thankfulness Circle

Gather children in a circle. If your group is larger than eight, make more than one circle. Have the first child tell something he or she is thankful for. Have the next child add a thought to the first idea. For example, if the first child says, "I'm thankful for my mom," the next child might say, "I'm thankful for my mom *and dad.*" The third child might say, "I'm thankful for my *beautiful* mom and dad." Go around the entire circle, with each child adding a new detail. Give each child a chance to add something to the first thanks.

Read Colossians 2:6-7 aloud. Say: **When we hear someone giving thanks, it reminds us of things that we can be thankful for, too. Letting others hear us being thankful is a way to strengthen one another in the faith we share. By the time we got to the last person in our circle, we truly were overflowing with thankfulness.**

- Which would you rather live with, criticism that grows with each person or thankfulness that grows with each person? Why?
- How can you start an atmosphere of thankfulness?
- Where can you start an atmosphere of thankfulness?
- When can you start an atmosphere of thankfulness?
- Why might you want to start an atmosphere of thankfulness?

Fast-Food Thanks

Make arrangements to take your group on a field trip. Explain that they will go to different places. At each place, they will stop to give thanks for something each place reminds them of. For example, if you take them to a fast-food restaurant, they might say they are thankful for daily food. If you take them to a cemetery, they might be thankful for heaven. At a nursing home, they might be thankful for a grandparent or for their own health.

Return to the meeting room, and have children sit in a circle. Have partners take turns sharing their reasons to be thankful. Read aloud Psalm 100. Ask:
- Where do you think "his gates" and "his courts" are?
- Where did you discover reasons to thank God?
- Could these ideas change the way you pray? How?

Close in a group prayer, thanking God for our blessings and asking God to make us aware of reasons to give thanks wherever we go.

The Silver Lining

Have each child think of a bad event—real or make-believe. Kids might say things such as, "a tornado in my room" or "pouring rain on the day of my baseball game." Then tell children to think of something good that could happen from the bad event. For example, kids might say, "Now I don't have to sweep my floor" or "Now my dad will be able to watch my rain-out game, 'cause he'll be back from his trip."

Help everyone find a partner. Explain that one person in each pair should name his or her bad event and the partner should respond by saying, "Oh no!" Then the child should answer, "That's OK, because now (fill in the good result)." Then partners should switch roles.

After completing this activity, have pairs join together to form four-somes. Have groups read 1 Thessalonians 5:18. Ask:

● Why is it sometimes hard to be thankful?

● How is it possible to be thankful all the time?

Read aloud Romans 8:28. Say: **Even though bad things happen, we can still give thanks to God because he can make something good out of bad things. Our job is to be on the lookout, just as you were in the activity we just did.** Close with prayer, asking the Lord to help us keep our eyes open for the good he brings into our lives.

Chapter Ten

Trust

Psychologists tell us that trust is foundational to all personality development. How well we learn to trust affects everything from how strong our relationships will be to how much energy we will have left for important tasks like learning. Maybe one reason God is known to us as our Father is because ideally, kids begin to learn trust from the care of loving parents. They can then easily transfer that trust to their relationships with God.

Far too many children today do not have that advantage. Their early experiences lead to distrust that threatens to undermine their futures. But we have a God who has a trustworthy plan. He is our safety net. Psalm 40 gives us the picture of God who lifts us from where we are and places us on a firm foundation: "Blessed is the man who makes the Lord his trust..." We need to assure kids that, even though people may fail them, God never will.

Use the activities in this chapter to help kids depend on God, recognize that they need to be trustworthy as God's representatives, and learn to identify people who can be trusted.

● ● ●

Taste and See

Before your meeting, prepare a tray of agreeable and disagreeable-tasting ingredients. For example, you could include baking chocolate, milk chocolate, baking powder, sugar, salt, jelly, and mustard.

Have kids form pairs. Give each pair two plastic spoons and a blindfold. Instruct one person in each pair to put the blindfold on. Say:

Some of the ingredients here taste good by themselves, but others taste awful. Your partner is going to feed you three samples of the ingredients from this tray. Your partner can choose to give you whichever samples he or she likes. Please remember that each of you gets a turn to be the one who feeds.

Instruct the children without the blindfolds to feed three samples of different ingredients to their partners. Have kids switch roles with their partners and repeat the process.

Have each pair combine with another pair to form groups of four. Have groups discuss these questions:

● **Did you trust your partner to give you good samples? Why or why not?**

● **Why did you choose to feed your partner what you did?**
Read Matthew 7:12.

● **What does this passage say about trust?**

● **Would you have fed your partner differently if you were trying to feed him or her like you'd like to be fed? Explain.**

● **Are you a trustworthy friend or an untrustworthy friend?**

Have kids return to their pairs to pray for each other. Encourage them to ask God to help them become more trustworthy and to help them treat others as they'd like to be treated.

Do You Trust Me?

Have kids form pairs, and give each pair a hard-boiled egg. Have each pair decorate its egg using colored markers. Then have each pair exchange its egg with another pair. Instruct pairs to play a toss game with the eggs by standing one arm's length away from each other and tossing the eggs back and forth. After both partners in each pair have tossed the egg, have both pairs take one step back and toss the egg again.

Encourage kids to continue this process until they are as far apart as they think they can throw the egg without breaking it. After a few eggs have broken, have each pair join with the pair who it exchanged eggs with to form groups of four. Have groups discuss these questions:

● **How did it feel to give your egg to another pair?**

● **How did it feel to get another pair's egg?**

● **Did you act responsibly with the other pair's egg? Explain.**

Read aloud Romans 12:10. Ask:

● **What would you have done with the egg if you were following the directions of this passage?**

● **Do you think you are a trustworthy person? Why or why not?**

● **Why is it important to be trustworthy?**

Have kids return to their pairs. Encourage each partner to share a time he or she was given something important to look after and acted responsibly and a time he or she was given something important to look after and acted irresponsibly. Ask:

● **How does it feel to fail someone when he or she puts trust in you?**

● **How does it feel to succeed when someone puts his or her trust in you?**

Tell kids that God wants them to be so trustworthy that others can depend on their devotion and willingness to put others' needs before their own.

On Your Head

Have kids form groups of three, and assign one of the following roles to each group member: a Fitter, a Pourer, and a Guinea Pig. Give each group a glass jar, a large rubber band, and piece of sheet-like material (test the material you use before this activity to make sure no water leaks). Instruct the Fitters to make "lids" for their jars by securing the material tightly over the tops of the jars and fastening it to the necks of the jars using the rubber bands (see diagram). Tell the Fitters to make certain the rubber bands are tightly secured to the jars.

Give each group a cup of water. Have the Pourer in each group use one finger to push down on the material in the middle of the top of the jar until his or her knuckle is level with the top of the jar. Tell the Pourers to slowly fill their jars with water by pouring it into the indentations they just created. Then have the Fitters make the lids very tight again.

Say: **Please don't try this yet—but if you turn the jar upside down, I believe all the water will stay inside.**

Ask:

● **How many of you believe me?**

● **How many of you are willing to allow the Pourer in your group to hold the jar upside down over your head for ten seconds? Why?**

Have the Guinea Pigs sit in chairs. Have the Pourers turn the jars over while standing away from the other children since some water may come out on the initial turning. Tell the Pourers that if the water from their jars doesn't continue to come out, they should hold the jars over the Guinea Pigs' heads while you count to ten. Quickly count to ten. Have groups discuss these questions:

● **Guinea Pigs, how did you feel about having the Pourers hold the jars over your heads?**

● **Did you think the material would stop the water from coming out of the jars? Why or why not?**

Read Proverbs 3:5 aloud, and ask:

● **When do you find it difficult to trust God? to trust others?**

● **How do we know we can trust God?**

Say: **You may have felt sure that the water was going to pour all over the Guinea Pigs' heads. But the wet material formed a seal. Sometimes it works that way with God. It may look to us as though there is no way we're going to be OK if we do what God tells us—like returning good for evil or forgiving someone who has wronged us. But God is greater than our understanding. We can trust God in every situation—even if it looks impossible to us.**

Trusting God's Guidance

Bring to class one road map for every four kids. When kids arrive, have them form groups of four and tell groups to look at their maps and plot a route between two cities you choose. Be sure the cities are far enough apart that plotting a route isn't too simple. If possible, allow kids to mark their chosen routes on the maps with markers.

When groups have plotted their routes, have them show and explain the routes they intend to take. Then ask:

● **Why do you think your route would work to get from place to place?**

● **Do you feel confident that the map shows the roads correctly? Why?**

● **How can you be sure the map isn't wrong?**

Say: **We often trust maps to guide us where we're going. But sometimes we trust other kinds of guidance. Let's see what kind of guidance Gideon trusted.**

Read aloud Judges 7:1-12, 16-22. Ask:

● **What was strange about the guidance God gave Gideon?**

● **What happened because Gideon trusted God's guidance?**

● **How is trusting God's guidance like trusting a road map?**

● **How do we receive guidance from God today?**

● **How do we know we can trust God's guidance?**

Say: **God gives us guidance through the Bible, through the Holy Spirit, and through other Christians. When we trust in God and the guidance he provides, we can know we'll succeed, just as Gideon did.**

Tough Times

Provide a plastic straw and a small- to medium-sized apple for each child plus one to demonstrate. Select a few volunteers to come up and try to push a straw through an apple. After three or four have failed, ask:

● **Do you think it is possible to push a straw through an apple? Why or why not?**

Then have children watch as you hold a straw with your thumb over the open upper end and thrust it quickly into an apple held in your other hand. (You may want to practice this in advance so that you avoid getting surprised by the core!) Push until the straw goes through. Then distribute straws, and let each child have a couple of tries on an apple. Have them save the apples for a later snack.

Gather the straws, and ask:

● **After the first few kids tried, did you think we'd ever get a straw through an apple? Why or why not?**

● **When things seem impossible, what are we tempted to do?**

Then say: **Let's look at someone in the Bible who was in what seemed to be an impossible situation.** Read Exodus 14:5-10 aloud. Then say: **The Israelites had the Red Sea in front of them and the Egyptian army coming after them. And they had no boats! They were trapped with no way of escape. But let's see what happened.** Read Exodus 14:13-28 aloud and then ask:

● **How did Moses and the Israelites get out of an impossible situation?**

● **Who did Moses trust to take care of them? Why?**

● **What should we do when we are in seemingly impossible situations today?**

Say: **God wants us to trust him the way Moses did. When we do, he'll take care of us just as he took care of Moses and the Israelites at the Red Sea.**

Blind Trust

Have the kids sit in a circle. Ask:

● **What is the most precious thing in your life?**

● **What if God told you to give it up? Would you trust him?**

Summarize the story of Isaac and Abraham. Say: **Here's a story of complete trust in God. Abraham and his wife Sarah wanted a child of their own very much. God promised to give them a child, and they trusted in God's promise even though Abraham and Sarah were very old—Abraham was one hundred and Sarah was ninety! Isaac was born to Abraham and Sarah, and they loved him dearly. Some time later, God wanted to test Abraham to make sure that Abraham still trusted in him. So he asked Abraham to do the ultimate act: to sacrifice his own beloved son!**

Read aloud Genesis 22:1-18.

Have the kids spread out around the room and sit on the floor facing the center of the room. One child will be chosen to accomplish a predetermined goal, such as picking up the hymnal in the corner of the room. Select a child, and blindfold him or her. Hold the child by the shoulder and turn him or her around a couple of times. The other children must then give short specific directions to help the blindfolded child accomplish the goal. For example, when you point to the first child, he or she might say, "Take three steps forward." The next child might say, "Turn to your right." Remind the children that they must help the blindfolded child not to run into any obstacles and to get to where he or she is going by giving one direction at a time. When the first child has completed the task, choose a new child and a new goal. Let as many children be blindfolded as you have time for.

After the game, talk about what it felt like to have to trust completely in someone else's directions, getting only a small part of the directions each time, and how this is a little like trusting in God to show us the way. Even though our players may have made mistakes, God's ways are perfect and he can always be trusted.

Web of Trust

Before class, find two poles or trees that can be used to support a web of yarn. Then create a web by entangling yarn between the poles or trees. It doesn't have to look like an actual spider web. Make the web with holes of various sizes and at different heights. Keep in mind the age, skill level, and size of your children, realizing that each child must go through a different hole.

Gather the children together in front of the web, and say: **Today we're going to play a game that requires trust, patience, and teamwork. It's called Spider Web. The object of the game is to not get caught in the web. You get caught in the web by touching it or by going through the same hole in the web more than once.** (You may have to allow children to use each hole twice or even three times, depending on the size of your group.) **We must all start on one side of the web and pass through the web without getting caught and without going through the same hole again. When we've gone through a hole, we'll tie a string on it so we know we can't use it again. We must each go through the web, so we should plan ahead so we know who will use each hole.**

Each person will take a turn getting through the web. Others must help by holding the web apart, giving a boost, or taking other creative measures. If a player touches the web, he or she must wait for another turn. After everyone has gone through the web, ask:

● **How did you feel as you were trying to pass through the web?**

● **How did you feel when you were helping others pass through the web?**

● **What does the word "trust" mean?**

● Who do you trust? Why do you trust them?

● How did this game involve trust?

Say: **The Bible is full of people who had trust in God. There is a story about three young men who trusted God to save their lives. Listen to what happened.** Read Daniel 3:16-28 aloud, and ask:

● **How was the men's trust like the trust you had during the Spider Web game?**

● **How is their trust different from the trust you had during the Spider Web game?**

● **What can these three young men teach us about trusting God?**

Complete your time together by having each child identify one way to trust God.

Mystery Trip

For this activity, take kids on a mystery trip. You'll need plenty of adult helpers and transportation. Be sure kids don't know where they're going, and be sure you have an impressive destination in mind so they won't be disappointed (the excitement will certainly build during the trip). For example, you may want to take children to the zoo, an amusement park, a favorite child-oriented restaurant, or a miniature golf course. Once they get there, allow kids to enjoy themselves for a while and then ask:

● **How did you feel as we were traveling here?**

● **What was it like to trust me that we were going to a place you would enjoy?**

● **How did you feel when we arrived here?**

Read Romans 15:13 aloud and then ask:

● **How was this mystery trip like trusting God?**

● **How can trusting God give you joy?**

Variation: If you can't take a trip with your kids, blindfold them and lead them throughout your church building. End up in a room that has been decorated and set up for a party. Be sure to include lots of snacks and fun party games!

Trust Me!

Make a long, curvy masking tape line on the floor that has a Start box at one end and a Home box at the other end.

Say: **Today we're going to play a board game called Trust Me! Guess what? You're going to be the board!** Choose two kids to be the first two Players, and have the rest of the class be the Spaces by lining up along the masking tape line.

Write each of the following on several index cards: 1, 2, 3, 4, 5, and King. Make enough cards so there's one for each child plus four or five extra. On the other side of each card, write the Space's response and how the Player will move. Use the following statements as examples:

1. Maybe you can trust me! Advance one space on your next turn.

2. You can trust me! Advance two spaces.

3. Don't trust me! Go back three spaces.

4. You can *really* trust me! Advance four spaces.

5. You shouldn't have trusted me! Return to Start, and draw again from the extra cards to begin your next turn.

King: Jesus is King! You can *always* trust God! You *and* the other Player advance all the way Home!

Shuffle the deck, and give one card to each Space, making sure kids don't reveal their cards. The Players will begin by each drawing a card from the leftover pile and advancing that number of Spaces. (If a Player draws a King, *both* Players automatically win the game and advance directly Home.) As the Players pass by each Space in the game board, they will each give that Space a high five.

After their initial moves, the Players move back and forth, based on what the Spaces say. A Player will ask the Space he or she "landed on" to reveal his or her card. Then the Space will say the corresponding statement and allow the Player to move accordingly.

A Player who reaches Home changes places with any Space so that everyone has a chance to be a Player. If Players exhaust the

draw pile, just reshuffle it. After a few kids have been Players, reshuffle the entire deck and deal out new cards to the Spaces.

Throughout the game, you can discuss these questions:
- **What does "trust" mean?**
- **How is this game like placing our trust in God?**
- **Who should we trust?**
- **Who shouldn't we trust?**
- **How do we know when to trust someone?**
- **Who can we always trust?**

Have younger kids simply move forward based on the card numbers. King cards will still take both Players all the way home. For older kids, yell "Shuffle!" during the game and let the Spaces find other spots on the masking tape line.

After every child has had a chance to be a Player, have the kids sit down as you read Psalm 115:9-13. Tell the kids God is someone we can *always* trust. Close in prayer, thanking God for his trustworthiness and asking for his wisdom in choosing friends who can be trusted.

Trust Is a Ticklish Thing

Ask the children to sit in a circle, surrounding you. It's important that you be within reaching distance of every child. Tell your children they're to obey a simple set of instructions:

1. Put your arms out in front of you, and clap your hands twice.
2. Raise your arms over your head, and clap your hands twice.
3. Hold your arms over your head until I tell you to drop your arms.

After you go through this set of instructions, ask one child to join you in the center of the circle. It's important that you've recruited and told this child what you'll do before you meet with all the children. Ask the child to not let anyone know what's coming.

Ask your "volunteer" to close his or her eyes and then go through the same routine. After the last instruction, reach over and tickle the child under his or her arms.

Then say: **I'd like you all to go through the steps we went through before—but this time, I'd like you to keep your eyes closed. No peeking! And keep those arms up while you wait for me to tell you to lower them.**

As you go through the steps, ask questions such as, "I wonder if everyone here is ticklish?" and "I wonder *how* ticklish everyone is?"

When you get to the step in which all the children have their arms over their heads, do nothing—but let suspense and tension build.

When twenty seconds have passed, ask children to open their eyes. Ask:

● **How did you feel doing this activity the first time? The second time?**

● **How easy or difficult was it for you to trust me the first time? The second time?**

● **Why did your feelings change?**

Say: **We trust people when we see they keep their word and we see they want to help us. When we lie, we become less trustworthy. So, if we lie to our parents, it makes it hard for them to trust us the next time we ask them to believe us. When we gossip about one friend, it makes it hard for our other friends to trust that we'll keep their secrets.**

God always keeps his word.

Ask a volunteer to read Psalm 22:3-5 aloud. Ask students to volunteer their answers to the following questions:

● **What's a promise God made to his people that he kept?**

● **What's a promise God made to us that he kept?**

● **What's a promise God made to us that we haven't yet seen fulfilled?** (Jesus' return)

● **Do you believe God is trustworthy? Why or why not?**

Say: **God is worthy of our trust. He has proven it by the way he has acted in the past. He wants us to keep our word like he has done so that when others look back at our record, they will know we are trustworthy, too.**

Who Ya Gonna Trust?

Ask children to place their hands in a large bowl of water that's very warm—but no warmer than 105 degrees Fahrenheit. At first, children will have to remove their hands from the water a few times before they're able to endure it. But soon, like a person getting accustomed to a very warm room, they'll be able to keep their hands in the bowl.

Explain that if you'd told the children they'd each be able to place their entire hand in the water, they wouldn't have believed you. Their feelings about the water changed as they got used to it.

Suggest an experiment. Ask children to each keep one hand in the hot water and put the other hand in a bowl of cold water. Ask kids to leave their hands in the bowls for one minute and then place both of their hands in a third bowl of lukewarm water. Ask them to quickly answer this question:

● **Is the water in this new bowl hot or cold?**

The third bowl will feel warm to the hand that's been in cold water and cold to the hand that's been in hot water.

Give children towels to dry their hands and then ask them to sit in a circle on the floor. Ask for a volunteer to read Proverbs 3:5-6 aloud. Ask:

● **What did you learn about your understanding of the temperature?**

● **What do you think it means to "lean not on your own understanding"?**

● **What's something you used to believe that you now know isn't true?**

Say: **Sometimes we can't trust our feelings. In the same way the third bowl of water felt both hot and cold and confused us, we can be confused by our feelings. But we can always trust God!**

Note: This activity may require more than one set of bowls, depending on the number of children in your class. Using large bowls, you can have a group of up to six per each set of bowls. Be sure the hot water is no warmer than 105 degrees Fahrenheit. Test the water's temperature with a thermometer, and never force a child to place his or her hand in the water! Add ice to the cold water to make it very cold.

Scripture Index

Group Publishing, Inc.
Attention: Product Development
P.O. Box 481
Loveland, CO 80539
Fax: (970) 669-1994

Evaluation for *Character Builders*

Please help Group Publishing, Inc., continue to provide innovative and useful resources for ministry. Please take a moment to fill out this evaluation and mail or fax it to us. Thanks!

● ● ●

1. As a whole, this book has been (circle one)

not very helpful   very helpful

1   2   3   4   5   6   7   8   9   10

2. The best things about this book:

3. Ways this book could be improved:

4. Things I will change because of this book:

5. Other books I'd like to see Group publish in the future:

6. Would you be interested in field-testing future Group products and giving us your feedback? If so, please fill in the information below:

Name _____

Street Address _____

City _____ State _____ Zip _____

Phone Number _____ Date _____

Exciting Resources for Your Children's Ministry

No-Miss Lessons for Preteen Kids

Getting the attention of 5th- and 6th-graders can be tough. Meet the challenge with these 22 faith-building, active-learning lessons that deal with self-esteem...relationships...making choices...and other topics. Perfect for Sunday school, meeting groups, lock-ins, and retreats!

ISBN 0-7644-2015-1

The Children's Worker's Encyclopedia of Bible-Teaching Ideas

New ideas—and lots of them!—for captivating children with stories from the Bible. You get over 340 attention-grabbing, active-learning devotions...art and craft projects...creative prayers...service projects... field trips...music suggestions...quiet reflection activities...skits...and more—winning ideas from each and every book of the Bible! Simple, step-by-step directions and handy indexes make it easy to slide an idea into any meeting—on short notice—with little or no preparation!

Old Testament   ISBN 1-55945-622-1
New Testament   ISBN 1-55945-625-6

"Show Me!" Devotions for Leaders to Teach Kids

Susan L. Lingo

Here are all the eye-catching science tricks, stunts, and illusions that kids love learning so they can flabbergast adults...but now there's an even *better* reason to know them! Each amazing trick is an illustration for an "Oh, Wow!" devotion that drives home a memorable Bible truth. Your children will learn how to share these devotions with others, too!

ISBN 0-7644-2022-4

Fun & Easy Games

With these 89 games, your children will *cooperate* instead of compete—so everyone finishes a winner! That means no more hurt feelings...no more children feeling like losers...no more hovering over the finish line to be sure there's no cheating. You get new games to play in gyms...classrooms...outside on the lawn...and as you travel!

ISBN 0-7644-2042-9

Order today from your local Christian bookstore, or write:
Group Publishing, P.O. Box 485, Loveland, CO 80539.